What to Do
When
Someone
You Love Is
Depressed

MITCH GOLANT, PH.D., AND SUSAN K. GOLANT, M.A.

Disciplining Your Preschooler and Feeling Good About It

Kindergarten: It Isn't What It Used to Be

Getting Through to Your Kids

Finding Time for Fathering

MITCH GOLANT, PH.D.

The Challenging Child (with DONNA CORWIN)

The Total Cancer Wellness Guide: Reclaiming Your Life after Diagnosis
(with KIM THIBOLDEAUX)

SUSAN K. GOLANT, M.A.

How to Have a Smarter Baby (with SUSAN LUDINGTON, PH.D.)

No More Hysterectomies (with VICKI HUFNAGEL, PH.D.)

The Joys and Challenges of Raising a Gifted Child

50 Ways to Keep Your Child Safe

Hardball for Women: Winning at the Game of Business (with PAT HEIM, PH.D.)

Kangaroo Care (with SUSAN LUDINGTON, PH.D.)

Taking Charge: How to Master the Eight Most Common Fears of Long-Term Illness
(with IRENE POLLIN, M.S.W.)

Helping Yourself Help Others: A Book for Caregivers (with ROSALYNN CARTER)

The Batterer: A Psychological Profile (with DON DUTTON, PH.D.)

Helping Someone with Mental Illness (with ROSALYNN CARTER)

Shyness: A Bold New Approach (with BERNARDO CARDUCCI, PH.D.)

Going to the Top (with CAROL GALLAGHER, PH.D.)

In the Company of Women
(with PAT HEIM, PH.D., AND SUSAN MURPHY, PH.D.)

You Don't Say (with AUDREY NELSON, PH.D.)

What to Do When Someone You Love Is Depressed

A Practical, Compassionate, and Helpful Guide

SECOND EDITION

MITCH GOLANT, Ph.D.,

and

SUSAN K. GOLANT

A Holt Paperback
Henry Holt and Company
New York

In memory of my mother and father

−M.C.G.

Holt Paperbacks
Henry Holt and Company, LLC
Publishers since 1866
175 Fifth Avenue
New York, New York 10010
www.henryholt.com

Distributed in Canada by H. B. Fenn and Company Ltd.

Grateful acknowledgment is made to Random House, Inc.,
and Don Congdon Associates, Inc., for permission to reprint
an excerpt from *Darkness Visible*, by William Styron.
Copyright © by William Styron. Rights throughout the British
Commonwealth are administered by Don Congdon Associates, Inc.,
New York. Reprinted by permission of Random House, Inc.,
and Don Congdon Associates, Inc.

Library of Congress Cataloging-in-Publication Data
Golant, Mitch.
  What to do when someone you love is depressed /
Mitch Golant and Susan K. Golant
    p. cm.
      Originally published: New York : Villard Books, 1996.
Includes bibliographical references. (p.)
ISBN-13: 978-0-8050-8277-7
ISBN-10: 0-8050-8277-8
1. Depression, Mental−Popular works.   2. Depressed persons−
Family relationships.   I. Golant, Susan K.   II. Title.
RC537.G62   1998   97-43348
616.85'27−dc21   CIP

Henry Holt books are available for special promotions and
premiums. For details contact: Director, Special Markets.

Originally published in hardcover in 1996 by Villard Books

First Holt Paperbacks Edition 2007

Designed by Deborah Kerner

Printed in the United States of America

7   9   10   8   6

" 'And feed your spirit hope and comfort; remember,
I won't abandon you in this nether sphere.' "

—DANTE,

The Inferno,

CANTO VIII, 101–102

Acknowledgments

WITHOUT THE INSPIRATION AND ENCOURAGEMENT of Villard's Suzanne Wickham-Beaird, we would not have had the opportunity to write such a book from the heart. We are deeply grateful to her, as we are to our agent, Bob Tabian, who always carefully oversees our interests.

There are many other people to thank. First are the professional colleagues who spurred us on with enthusiasm for this project, thoughtfully adding their insights and experiences. These include Alan Rabinowitz, M.S.W.; Malcolm Schultz, J.D., M.A.; Michael States, M.A.; Stuart Wolman, M.D.; and especially William Coburn, Ph.D., and Linda Marsa, M.A. I'm grateful to my colleagues: Cheryl Benun, Ph.D., Phyllis Gelber, Ph.D., Barbara Guggenheim, Ph.D., Anne Panofsky, Ph.D., and Alan Solomon, Ph.D., for their professional integrity.

My mentor, teacher, and friend, Harold H. Benjamin, Ph.D., founder and president of the Wellness Community-National, taught me the power of the written word to make a difference in the world. Harold led by example, demanding no less of himself than he asked of others.

I am grateful to my family—our daughters, Cherie and Aimee, who in wholeheartedly living their lives bring us great joy and love. I owe much to my brother, William Golant, and my in-laws, Mary and Arthur Kleinhandler and Henriette Kleinhandler, who are always there for me when I need them.

Finally, to Susan, my wife and co-author. We are as close as cell mitosis—best friends, lovers, confidants. You are a comfort in times of sorrow and a defender in times of strife. An incisively passionate writer, thinker, and teacher, you help so many give birth to their life's work. This, of course, includes me.

Deep in my heart I believe that in writing this book, we have helped each other repair so many wounds. We have given dignity to my parents' lives in hopes that their suffering would be transformed into a source of comfort to others.

Acknowledgments for
the Second Edition

We are grateful for the hundreds of e-mails and notes that we have received from our readers over the years—sharing with us the aid and comfort that our book has provided them. In truth, they are the inspiration and motivation for this revised edition. In addition, I would like to thank Andy Roth, M.D., and Christine Forest, M.D., for their insights, edits, and ideas about state-of-the-art psychopharmacological care. Their compassion and creativity are an inspiration. We are also grateful to our editors at Holt, Flora Esterly and Lindsay Ross, for their enthusiasm and support.

—M.C.G.

Contents

PART I

Understanding Depression

◆

CHAPTER 1

When Someone You Love Is Depressed

WHEN SOMEONE YOU LOVE IS DEPRESSED . . .

. . . you feel lost, afraid, confused.

. . . you long for the person who was.

. . . you don't recognize who he or she has become.

. . . you feel shut out.

. . . you feel angry and frustrated.

. . . you feel drained.

. . . you are desperate for a way to connect.

. . . you feel guilty and alone.

. . . you will do anything to help.

When someone you love is depressed, you may experience a wide range of emotions such as these, and more. You may feel shock. You might wish to push away the whole situation and deny reality. You could be angry. "How could this happen?" you may thunder. "Why is this happening to us, to our family, to my friend?" You might withdraw or feel hopeless and depressed yourself. You might even try negotiating with God or with your loved one: "If only you would try harder . . . If only you would get up in the morning, I'll be more responsive to you."

Your loved one may have become depressed because of having just lost a job or experienced a financial setback, or may be dejected because of a recent death in the family or the breakup of a relationship. There is a continuum between simply having the blues to suffering from a full-blown clinical depression. My family's story falls toward the more difficult end of the spectrum. I share it now as a way to convey how deeply felt is the caregiver's struggle to help a depressed loved one and the genuine pain that the depressed individual suffers.

When I was fourteen years old, my mom became depressed. My mother's depression, precipitated by my older brother's departure to England for graduate studies at Oxford University, felt as if a blackout shade had dropped first over her room and then the entire house. There had been episodes of depression before, like partial eclipses of the sun, which had thrown us off balance for a few moments. But in the past, after the shadow had receded, we were all able to get back on track.

This was different. For days and then weeks, my mom would not leave her room. Her every breath was a moan of pain. She wore only black nightclothes. She rarely dressed. Somehow dinner would appear—but she didn't. The aloneness was deafening.

I remember trying to help. I'd go into her room after school and sit at the edge of her bed, hoping to cheer her with stories about my friends' schoolyard antics. I'd leave tests that I was proud of on the nightstand. She didn't respond. Sometimes I found myself just talking to her, pretending that she was listening . . . and acting lighthearted. In truth, I was terrified—it was all I could do to keep from bursting.

At other times she would rant. It would start rather quietly, and at first I was thankful she was speaking. But soon her tone would turn surly and hard as she went on about some person or event that had ruined her life. She threatened suicide. Sometimes *I* was the "cause" of her problems.

No amount of protestation or reasoning would penetrate that drawn shade of despair.

My father sought help. Our family doctor would make timely home visits. On occasion my mother responded positively to this show of concern. But sometimes after the doctor left she would rail at us for embarrassing her and aggravating the situation. My mom was ashamed that our doctor would think she was "crazy," and as a result she refused any treatment except pain pills. She would use various prescribed medications for the many physical complaints that became the focus of her problems. After several months of this roller coaster of silence, ranting, physical complaints, and outright rejection, my dad retreated and my grades and achievement started to suffer.

My mother was never quite the same.

Many years later, while in graduate school, studying educational psychology, I decided to test the waters of psychotherapy and train as a hot-line counselor for the Los Angeles Suicide Prevention Center. During the interview, one of the directors asked, "Why do you have an interest in suicide prevention?" I hemmed and hawed, cleared my throat, started talking about "helping others" and always having been "interested in psychology." I mentioned in passing that my mother had been depressed at times.

At the end of the interview, the director said, "I think the best reason you offered for doing this training is that it might help you understand your mother. Her depression is a good reason for your engaging in this work. In fact, it makes you highly qualified. That's excellent training!"

With that surprising introduction began a long road to understanding my mother's depression and, in the process, helping myself become a better son, a more sensitive caregiver, and a more empathetic psychologist. What I didn't know then—but what the director had seen so clearly during the interview—was that my interest in psychology was motivated by my need to find ways to help my mom, my family, and myself.

What motivates me now is to share with you what I've learned about how to cope when someone you love is depressed. What I have discovered from years of training and from having counseled hundreds of families who have shared their sorrows and their joys is that there are ways you can help someone you love who is depressed. And in that process, you will grow closer.

THE MYTHS SURROUNDING DEPRESSION

Unlike chronic illnesses such as heart disease or arthritis, depression carries with it a stigma of shame that adds to its intensity. This stigma can prevent the 20 million Americans who suffer from depression—and who desperately need treatment—from seeking help. Indeed, according to a report in *The New York Times,* two thirds of those requiring treatment for depression never receive it.

Untreated depression costs the nation between $30 billion and $44 billion a year in medical expenses, work absenteeism, and lost productivity.

The myths and half-truths that abound concerning this condition may make it even harder for you and your loved one to cope with an illness that in itself can be terribly debilitating. Let's look at some of these myths right now, and dispel them.

MYTH 1:
WITH ENOUGH WILLPOWER, ANYONE CAN OVERCOME DEPRESSION.

Statements such as "If only he would try harder . . ." or "If only she would be reasonable . . ." or "If only he would snap out of it!" can exacerbate an already difficult situation.

Expressing such sentiments to a person who is depressed is as futile as telling a kidney-disease patient, "With enough willpower you can control your renal functioning."

The belief that he lacks the fortitude and character to overcome his problem can reinforce the negative thoughts a depressed person already has about himself, and can cause him to label himself weak, lazy, stupid, or a failure. This is counterproductive, for it potentially deepens the downward spiral of self-criticism and despair that is already at work.

Even those of us who are not depressed are familiar with self-critical thoughts. We all have them. But we know they come and go, and usually we can manage them. Unfortunately, a depressed person is unable to do so; controlling his negative thoughts is not within the realm of what he feels is possible. The words repeat endlessly like a mournful refrain on a broken record: "I'm lazy," "I'm stupid," "I'm a failure," "I'm worthless," "Life is hopeless."

Often a depressed person, as if in a free fall, goes where his emotions take him. Those of us who are not depressed know that the rides our emotions take us on eventually end, but the depressed individual experiences the ups and downs, twists and turns of his feelings as if on a runaway train without a clear sense of how or when—or even if—he can ever get off. Unfortunately, he can't will himself off, either.

Depression is an illness that has biological, social, psychological, and genetic components. It must be treated. It may often be a chronic condition that comes and goes, with flare-ups and moments of remission. Willpower has little to do with it.

MYTH 2:
IT'S ALL IN HIS HEAD.

Some years ago I watched the movie *The Madness of King George*. I remember thinking as I sat in the theater, "Oh, King George is depressed. It must be because he lost the Colonies. The doctor is using his eighteenth-century version of positive reinforcement . . . and it's working."

Even I was taken aback during the final credits when I learned of the medical condition—porphyria, a physical illness of the nervous system—that might have triggered the king's madness. I wondered, was King George's problem only physical or was the loss of the Colonies a significant stressor that triggered the illness? Who knows?

But the movie's lesson is crucial for all of us. What looks like madness may in reality be the consequences of some biological condition. Depression is not always in the head. It can, in fact, occur as a symptom of a seemingly unrelated medical ailment.

MYTH 3:
DEPRESSION IS SOMETHING TO BE ASHAMED OF.

Some people, like my mother, believe that depression is a form of craziness, and this belief evokes shame. This hearkens back to the state of affairs a mere century ago and calls up images that still tenaciously resonate within us today, of individuals experiencing emotional illness who were shunned in society and thrown into inhumane lunatic asylums.

Shame is a symptom that often accompanies depression. However, it simply isn't true that depression is something to be ashamed of. Depression is not a moral stand one takes by choice, a choice for which one should blame oneself.

As a symptom, however, the depressed person's feelings of shame can be a valuable part of understanding some of the psychological roots of the illness. Once these feelings are explored in therapy, it often relieves some of the depression. But labeling depression as a shameful state makes it even worse—like heaping shame upon shame.

Unfortunately, someone who is depressed may at times also think, feel, and even believe that he is going crazy. When you add to the shame the stigma of craziness, the situation becomes dizzying. The association with craziness conjures up images straight out of *One Flew over the Cuckoo's Nest,* in which institutionalization is followed, horribly, by electroconvulsive therapy administered without anesthesia and lobotomy. These may be unrealistic and outmoded fears, but for the person who is depressed, they are quite real.

As a caregiver, your role is to be a supportive and strengthened ally, reassuring your loved one that his worst fears won't be realized, and that you will be there through all the treatments.

We all must be careful not to label, stereotype, or pigeonhole anyone suffering from depression.

MYTH 4:
YOU CAN'T BE PRODUCTIVE
IF YOU'RE DEPRESSED.

Wrong again! An individual can be depressed and still function. Most people who are depressed *and are receiving treatment* (psychotherapy, with or without drug therapy) live productive lives. They carry out family responsibilities. That's the wonder of medication and psychological treatment. People in treatment who are depressed work at their jobs in a similar manner to a professional football player who plays with pain and injury. They just push through it. And each day is a small victory.

One of my clients, Sarah, who was in her early thirties, had moved to Los Angeles from the East Coast after having graduated at the top of her class from an Ivy League school. Her new job, as a computer analyst, was exciting for the first year. She received outstanding performance reviews and a handsome bonus at the end of the year.

The next year, however, Sarah was devastated. Her boss was transferred and she was shifted to a different team and project. She suddenly became the odd woman out. This triggered her depression. As the pressures at her job worsened and her depression deepened, her job actually became her lifeline; she made sure that she went to work every day and thus maintained some control over her life.

The idea behind treatment is to enhance your loved one's ability to act in the world *despite* the depression.

MYTH 5:
THERAPY DOESN'T WORK.

Therapy for depression is highly effective in 70 percent of cases, and untold benefits derive from treatment. It enhances productivity and quality of life. In fact, a *New York Times* article reporting on a survey of various regimens for depression supports the use of psychotherapy. The psychologist Dr. David Antonuccio and his colleagues at the University of Nevada School of Medicine in Reno found in their research that "despite the conventional wisdom, the data suggest that there is no stronger medicine than psychotherapy in the treatment of depression, even if severe."

Interestingly, *Consumer Reports* reached similar conclusions. After four thousand of its subscribers responded to the largest-ever survey on the use of therapy and/or drugs to treat depression, researchers at the Consumers Union determined that "psychotherapy alone worked as well as psychotherapy combined with medication, like Prozac or Xanax. Most people who took the drugs did feel they were helpful, but many people reported side effects."

Sometimes, however, therapy alone may not be enough. If your loved one is severely depressed, he may require medication along with psychotherapy.

MYTH 6:
MEDICATIONS ARE ADDICTIVE OR AT LEAST CREATE A DEPENDENCY.

Addiction carries with it symptoms of withdrawal and the implication that once hooked on a drug, one can never kick the habit. Dependency means that one needs more and more of a substance in order for it to have its full effect. Underlying this is the fear of overdosing. None of these conditions occur with most of the modern medications used to treat depression.

It is true, however, that an individual who has experienced several bouts of severe depression may need to take medication for the rest of his life, as a life- and sanity-saving measure. Whatever the circumstances, medications should be constantly monitored for proper dosage, frequency of use, and palliative effect. We'll delve more deeply into medications in Chapter 7.

MYTH 7:
DEPRESSION IS THE SAME FOR EVERYONE.

"Depression" is often used as a catchall term for many different problems and states ranging from normal sadness from the loss of a loved one to self-destructive, suicidal behavior. (In Chapter 2, I will cover the various degrees of depression, including "clinical depression.")

But depression is certainly not a single ailment. It can be

- the result of other problems, including drug addiction and alcoholism
- linked to certain conditions like Parkinson's disease, attention deficit disorder (ADD), thyroid deficiency (hypothyroidism), hepatitis, multiple sclerosis, arthritic conditions, benign brain tumors, some cancers and their treatments, premenstrual syndrome, and the recent birth of a baby
- a symptom of infection with certain viruses such as those causing mononucleosis, Epstein-Barr syndrome, chronic fatigue syndrome, AIDS, and even the flu
- a side effect of medications such as birth-control pills, certain blood-pressure-lowering drugs, and cortisone

Depression can also manifest itself in many forms:

- deep melancholy
- pessimism
- anger
- fatigue
- anxiety
- eating disorders
- compulsive or addictive behaviors such as gambling, sexual addiction, or alcoholism
- acting out in children or adolescents
- in the case of manic-depression (also called bipolar illness), super-high-charged activity followed by periods of numbing lethargy and despondency

The important thing to remember is that psychological, social, biological, and genetic elements must be addressed—diagnosed and treated—before your loved one can have a clear plan of action. In Chapter 2, we'll cover more completely the nature of depression.

MYTH 8:
SUBSTANCE ABUSE AND DEPRESSION ARE UNRELATED.

On the contrary, substance abuse and depression are highly related. According to Alan I. Leshner, former director of the National Institute on Drug Abuse, 25 percent of all individuals who have major depression also have a diagnosable substance-abuse problem.

There is a circular relationship between substance abuse and depression. Many alcoholic or drug-addicted individuals are actually attempting to self-medicate their depression when they indulge in these substances. For example, if they are manic-depressive, they may use alcohol to soften their highs and cocaine to resurrect them from their lows. My mother's drugs of choice were sleeping pills and Empirin-Codeine No. 3, an addictive painkiller that she believed would numb her emotional agony.

Unfortunately, however, these are only temporary solutions. The initial effect of alcohol, for example, is to help the depressed individual feel relieved. It is a disinhibitor—it frees one of one's inhibitions—but it is also a depressant. So while the alcohol may make your loved one feel better at first, its eventual effect will be to deepen his depression. With highly addictive substances such as cocaine or codeine, the cravings can create more complex problems still.

Proper use of antidepressant medications often helps in the management and alleviation of substance abuse and other addictive behaviors. Paul, a client of mine, had multiple addictions to pornography, food, marijuana, and alcohol. Once his depression was diagnosed and treated, the addictions, which were a tremendous drain on his productivity and his family, became much more manageable.

THE USUAL RESPONSE

When someone we love is depressed, I have found that the first response is usually disbelief. We can't fathom what has happened. We search for what might have triggered the episode. We are angry and frustrated. We are in shock.

But for the person who is depressed, the dark mood has been a fire smoldering internally for a long time. The precipitating event—the issue that seems to have triggered the depression—is often the blast of air that whips the embers into a firestorm. For my mother, it was my brother's departure; for others it can be the loss of a job or a loved one, a business failure, the diagnosis of a chronic illness, a divorce—any loss that seems overwhelming.

We might look at the precipitating event and believe that it is the whole cause rather than recognizing that elements of the depression—the lack of productivity, the negative thoughts, the sleepiness or sleeplessness, the lack of appetite, the bouts of sluggishness or accelerated activity—already existed in a more muted form all along. Perhaps they seemed like idiosyncrasies rather than an indication of smoldering problems. Or perhaps the depressed person had simply been keeping the depth of these problems to himself.

An apparently sudden explosion of symptoms—including something as serious as a suicidal gesture like overdosing on pills or slashing wrists—might cause us to blame ourselves for what has happened.

Many family members and loved ones believe that they "should have seen it coming," or that they "waited too long," before seeking help. At this stage they may engage in a great deal of activity to fix the problem. The family and the depressed individual run to the physician, consult with psychiatrists, reconnect with a therapist from a previous flare-up. There is a tremendous expenditure of energy to correct the problem, almost as if it were a burst water pipe that simply needs to be patched.

Of course, it is important to seek help and mobilize your resources, but you have to learn to pace yourselves. You can't expect the problem to be resolved immediately. Remember, when a water pipe breaks, the leak it causes can stain walls, ruin carpets, warp floors, even undermine the ground upon which a house is built. There is much work to do. Patience is essential at this stage, and it's best to focus on the value of your efforts and small successes.

In the case of my own family, lacking adequate resources, my father got stuck in withdrawal and hopelessness. I remember seeing him sitting at the edge of my mother's bed, putting his arm on her leg or holding her hand. Later at night, I'd see him desolate, a shot of whiskey in his hand, staring into space . . . tired . . . wondering how he would get up early the next morning to go to work, how he could face another day. He was lost in his aloneness, not knowing what to do.

Slowly, feeling despondent himself, he began withdrawing from my mother. He would start for work earlier and earlier each morning and come home later and later each night, leaving my mother even more isolated . . . leaving himself and me even more alone.

My father was somehow sucked into the maelstrom of my mother's illness. With proper guidance, he could have found ways to help himself and my mom. *What to Do When Someone You Love Is Depressed* will help you find a way together through the illness toward light. You want to maintain your relationship; you want to be helpful. This book will enhance your ability to reach those goals.

ON HELPING

One of the purposes of *What to Do When Someone You Love Is Depressed* is to support you and your loved one to get and give help. The problem may be that the depressed person is too immobilized to seek help for himself. Yet many treatments are available for depression, and most are quite effective.

Think of it this way. If you have a recurring headache, sometimes all it takes is a nap to clear it away. At other times, a nap and two aspirin will do the trick. If that doesn't work, you might take Tylenol or Advil. You take the day off too. Failing that, you see the doctor, and maybe get neurological tests or try biofeedback. You go on vacation. You even change jobs, if you have to. You move to another city. In other words, you do whatever you must.

The same can be said in approaching a solution to depression. You keep searching for the most effective treatment. It's best not to become attached to any one approach as if it were *the answer.* Support the depressed person in all of his efforts—encourage even the smallest steps he may be taking.

That's what happened with Sarah, the client of mine who became depressed when her job situation deteriorated. Her husband, Frank, was her biggest cheerleader and helper. He facilitated getting her résumés out to other firms. He even helped her to document her poor treatment in the workplace.

Flexibility, pragmatism, and the techniques offered in subsequent chapters will help you devise a survival and recovery strategy. They are your arsenal; use them when they work but discard them if they lose their effectiveness. Fine-tune them to your personality and situation.

It is important also for you to recognize that there is a limit to how much you can help. A person who is depressed must take control of the illness in order to begin to heal. There is a fine line be-

tween being helpful and being an enabler—someone who pr_
the depressed person from solving his problems himself, ther
allowing them to go untreated. His taking responsibility for ed_
cating himself, his active participation in fighting the disease, and
his acknowledgment of the depth of the illness are critical in his recovery. We will discuss this further in Chapter 4, "Your Role as
Strengthened Ally."

Still, there are things you can do and say, attitudes that you can
hold, boundaries and limits that you can establish that are more
helpful than the ones my parents chose. Even if your actions don't
appear to register with your loved one at first, they do. They are the
correct and most helpful things to do.

Moreover, there are ways of comforting and taking care of yourself in the process.

When someone you love is depressed, you need not feel despair. There is hope.

◆

CHAPTER 2

What Is
Depression?

A PERSON WHO EXPERIENCES SADNESS OR HAS THE blues may call her state depression, but she may not be technically depressed. There is a continuum of emotional experience that ranges from a simple case of the blues to a full-blown clinical depression.

NORMAL SADNESS

Margaret, a fifty-two-year-old attorney, came into my office one afternoon complaining about feeling depressed. "I'm so sad," she said. "I can't seem to get involved in anything I do. I just don't have the energy."

Knowing that Margaret's youngest child had just left for her freshman year at college, I probed a bit.

"Are you having trouble sleeping?" I asked.

"Why, no," Margaret replied, surprised that I would ask.

"And have you noticed any changes in your appetite?"

"God, I wish I did. I can't seem to lose any weight at all!" she said.

I pursued more questions about Margaret's relationships with her husband, friends, and colleagues. And I asked if she had experienced any persistent, despairing thoughts about death or dying.

"No," Margaret replied, almost indignantly.

I sat back, a bit relieved. Margaret's empty nest had given her a case of the blues. Even though she said she was depressed, in clinical terms she was not. As we went on to discuss what her daughter's absence meant to her, I felt confident that Margaret would make the adjustments necessary and pull out of her funk in a week or two.

It's important not to confuse sadness owing to grief and loss with depression. Sadness is often a response to a recent external event, such as an injury or illness or loss of a loved one. It's situational. The vast majority of us will experience it at one time or another in our lives; we go through it as a phase.

For example, I remember when the space shuttle *Challenger* exploded. Like everyone else in the nation, I was deeply disturbed by this tragic accident, but I was particularly moved by the death of the high school teacher and mother Christa McAuliffe, the one civilian astronaut on board, whose motto "I touch the future; I teach" moved me deeply. I felt sad all week and cried at times, identifying with her family as well as with the families of the others who were lost.

As the days and weeks passed, I waxed philosophical about how our lives are transitory—we think that we are in control, but everything can change in a moment. I wondered whether the mission was really a failure, or whether perhaps these brave men and women, despite the explosion, were still successful. After all, they were only in control of their efforts, not the outcome of the mission. I hoped that from the wreckage of the shuttle, NASA could find the cause of the accident and thereby prevent future tragedies. Somehow, I attempted to find the value and higher purpose to the astronauts' suffering and the nation's pain.

After several weeks, as other events in my personal life began to crowd in, the fate of the *Challenger* and her crew faded from my immediate consciousness, and so did my sadness.

Similarly, my client Margaret's sadness was linked to a particular event—her daughter's departure and the loss of her role as mother. Eventually, however, she would discover that her newfound freedom would allow her to devote even greater energy to her excellent relationship with her husband and her flourishing career. As her sadness dissipated, she became excited by the thought of all she could accomplish, now that she was no longer responsible for overseeing her children's welfare on a daily basis.

The purpose of this chapter is to provide an important tool to help someone you love who has the blues or is depressed. I will delineate the symptoms of depression so that you can distinguish this illness from the blues, or everyday sadness. Many excellent authors have written about their depressions and about the impossibility for anyone not suffering from this illness to truly comprehend the devastation it wreaks on the human soul, and I will share some of their writings with you.

In this chapter, I will educate you about the elements of depression so that you can better understand your loved one's experience, thereby becoming a partner in her fight for recovery. And if it is just the blues and not clinical depression, you'll find out why this state, too, should not be ignored.

THE BLUES–DEPRESSION CONTINUUM

Sadness such as Margaret's is one of the normal emotions that we all feel. Sadness, disappointment, loss, grief, and mourning—like joy, satisfaction, accomplishment, and elation—are among myriad feelings that are normal, depending on the situations in which we find ourselves. Usually, the blues, much like our other emotions, dissipate in time.

But there are occasions when the blues can become depression. When and how that happens usually depends upon how much one ruminates on one's state. Rumination is repetitive worry—brooding thoughts that fixate on how poorly one is doing or how sad one is feeling.

Connie's story helps demonstrate how the blues can grow into a full depression. Connie was a thirty-year-old high school history teacher. In her five years of teaching, she had been quite successful, creating innovative lesson plans that motivated her students to go beyond mere textbook learning. Her skill and dedication as a teacher earned her the near-universal praise of her students, their parents, and the school's administrators.

When Connie came to see me, however, she complained about losing sleep and worrying about her declining productivity. She now spent hours thinking about how to conduct her classes, but she somehow couldn't put her plans on paper or into action. What's more, the reports her students had slaved over just sat in a heap on her desk week after week. She had planned how she would divide the stack into piles of ten and attack the work over several long weekends, but somehow, she just couldn't bring herself to do it.

Always a high achiever, Connie was unused to this slump. Soon, she began calling herself lazy. "What's wrong with me?" she wondered out loud in the therapy session. "Why can't I get myself to finish anything?"

As she continued to talk, it became clear that Connie had sustained several significant losses during the previous year. She had broken off a long-term relationship with her boyfriend, and the supportive principal who had mentored her had transferred to another school. Either of these losses could have been responsible for Connie's blues and her slowed productivity.

But her ruminations—those internal questions regarding her competence, laziness, and overall self-worth—were edging her toward depression. Science writer Daniel Goleman explains in his book *Emotional Intelligence,* "One of the main determinants of whether a depressed mood will persist or lift is the degree to which people ruminate. Worrying about what's depressing us, it seems, makes the depression all the more intense and prolonged."

Connie's ruminations about work seemed to divert her attention from the emotional pain she experienced elsewhere in her life. If she had continued without treatment, the ruminations and worry might have become even more intense. She might have tossed and turned night after night, agonizing about what her students and their parents were thinking of her. She might have become troubled by thoughts of being fired. She might have brooded about her waning appetite and inability to focus. And if these ruminations had persisted and intensified, she might have fallen from a simple case of the blues into a full-blown depression.

Clearly, the blues are a mood we should take seriously. Although it is not depression, it is a step along the continuum that can lead toward depression. In Connie's case, the decision to get treatment early to break the pattern of negative thoughts helped prevent a bad case of the blues from becoming a clinical depression.

CLINICAL DEPRESSION FROM THE INSIDE OUT

Kay Redfield Jamison, a professor of psychiatry at Johns Hopkins University who suffers from manic-depressive disorder, writes in *An Unquiet Mind: A Memoir of Moods and Madness,* "Others imply that they know what it is like to be depressed because they have gone through a divorce, lost a job, or broken up with someone. But these experiences carry with them feelings. Depression, instead, is flat, hollow, and unendurable."

Sometimes the sadness following the death of a loved one can be debilitating. The mourner seems to act and react in slow motion. But this period of grieving is to be expected and is not a mental disorder. If the bereavement is not excessive or prolonged, a period of withdrawal and sorrowing can help one recover from a crushing blow. (If the days of mourning stretch into weeks and then months, however, you must suspect depression.) "Grief," Kay Jamison writes, "fortunately, is very different from depression; it is sad, it is awful, but it is not without hope."

True depression, on the other hand, is not necessarily linked to obvious external events, such as a death or the loss of a job. As we shall see, it can be associated with one's genetic heritage and a chemical imbalance in the brain. And it doesn't come and go. It's not simply a bad mood that can be shaken off in a week or two.

People who are depressed describe the experience as a soul-crushing sense of hopelessness and despair—as if they have no self. Everything they see, feel, and endure has been tinted and tainted by a dark cloud. Trees and flowers in the springtime, which for the rest of us would seem symbols of hopefulness and loveliness, can evoke images of decay and disintegration in a depressed person. Indeed, she may feel as if she were drowning in a sense of self-loathing and unrelenting pain, and may constantly ruminate on death and suicide.

Jamison writes about what it feels like to be depressed:

[Depression] bleeds relationships through suspicion, lack of confidence and self-respect, the inability to enjoy life, to walk or talk normally, the exhaustion, the night terrors, the day terrors. . . . It gives you the experience of how it must be to be old, to be old and sick, to be dying; to be slow of mind; to be lacking in grace, polish, and coordination; to be ugly; to have no belief in the possibilities of life, the pleasures of sex, the exquisiteness of music, or the ability to make yourself and others laugh.

These negative thoughts remain day in and day out, pervading the individual's life. Often, however, they are kept secret from family, friends, and colleagues until, like spores—dormant till they find themselves in the proper environment—they seem to erupt as the result of a precipitating event.

THE RANGE OF DEPRESSIVE EMOTIONS

Depression doesn't always look the same; it can manifest itself as a range of emotions. Those who are depressed can move from anxiety to anger to withdrawal, and then back again. Like my mother, your loved one may even experience all of these emotions in one episode.

Each person is unique. You may find that your loved one will feel or express one emotion more than another. For example, my mother's anger would erupt first. Usually, that eventually led to withdrawal. Her anxiety would manifest itself when a holiday, birthday, or celebration required her to be with others. On those occasions she was afraid of their disapproval. She worried that she didn't look good enough or wasn't dressed well enough.

One of my patients, Claire, described how in the morning she felt fine. This would lead her to hope and believe that the depression had lifted. However, by four o'clock in the afternoon, she would find herself becoming more and more anxious. Her ruminations about her mounting anxiety would trigger another depressive episode.

CONCEALING THE DEPRESSION

Karen, another client whose youngest child left for college, also came to see me complaining of depression. When I interviewed her, I found that six months earlier, Karen's mother had died after a long battle with lung cancer, but symptoms of depression, such as insomnia and loss of interest in sexual intimacy (indeed, now even being touched felt oppressive to her), had bothered Karen for a year prior to her mother's death. Her son's departure for school was the final straw.

This woman was truly depressed. She could barely find the strength to get up each morning and face the day. She was overwhelmed with thoughts of death. Yet she hadn't shared her anguish with her husband or sister, the two people in the world she most relied on for support. Asking for help seemed foreign to her. Like so many other depressed individuals, she suffered in silence.

Why do people keep their symptoms a secret? Perhaps, like the Pulitzer Prize–winning novelist William Styron, they do not realize what they're dealing with. In *Darkness Visible: A Memoir of Madness,* the 1990 chronicle of his depression, Styron writes:

> *I did notice that my surroundings took on a different tone at certain times: the shadows of nightfall seemed more somber, my mornings*

were less buoyant, walks in the woods became less zestful, and there
was a moment during my working hours in the late afternoon when
a kind of panic and anxiety overtook me. . . . It should have been
plain to me that I was already in the grip of a mood disorder, but I
was ignorant of such a condition at that time.

Others believe that the symptoms will go away "tomorrow," if they take a walk, a nap, a shot of whiskey, another pill. But the to-morrows stretch on and on. When friends notice their apparent ex-haustion, some depressed people respond with "Oh, I'm fine. Don't worry about me." Yet all the while, inside, they too are ques-tioning their condition. As Kay Jamison explains, "You're fright-ened, and you're frightening, and you're 'not at all like yourself but will be soon,' but you know you won't."

There is an element of self-preservation in this denial. We're used to thinking that we're strong enough to handle all the prob-lems that come our way. It's a sign of weakness if we can't, so we avoid acknowledging that we can't cope. But for the depressed in-dividual, eventually there is no shaking the negative thoughts.

"The gray drizzle of horror induced by depression takes on the quality of physical pain," Styron writes. "But it is not an immedi-ately identifiable pain, like that of a broken limb. It might be more accurate to say that despair . . . comes to resemble the diabolical discomfort of being imprisoned in a fiercely overheated room. And because no breeze stirs this cauldron, because there is no es-cape from this smothering confinement, it is entirely natural that the victim begins to think ceaselessly of oblivion."

Clearly, though some of the symptoms of the blues can overlap with those of depression, it is not the same condition at all. After a while, if the symptoms become severe enough, they can no longer be concealed.

HOW DEPRESSION IS DIAGNOSED

Depression is called a mood, or affective, disorder. "Affective" refers to feelings and emotions. It is an illness that directly impacts an individual's entire being. It alters and disrupts one's mood, one's thoughts, one's body, and one's behavior. Let's look at these more closely.

MOOD

As I explained above, a depressed individual is subject to low moods. She may lose interest in activities that she usually enjoys. In *Prozac Nation: Young and Depressed in America,* Elizabeth Wurtzel describes the state as "pure dullness, tedium straight up," and uses words such as "slowness" and "dreariness" to describe her moods.

The depressed individual may also seem worried, melancholy, or generally down in the dumps. These moods may or may not be linked to actual events, but if they are, as in my client Karen's case, they seem out of proportion to what one would usually expect; they are more persistent and more severe.

THOUGHTS

Stubbornly negative, hopeless thoughts about the present and future predominate during depression. These can be mixed with preoccupations with death and suicide. The depressed individual feels alone, inadequate, hopeless, and worthless and will be pessimistic about almost everything. As Karen, deep in the throes of such thoughts, explained, "It's that I'm *incapable* of thinking about anything else that makes it so scary and futile."

The depressed person may also have trouble concentrating, staying focused, remembering, and making decisions. Because of this, in an older person, the confusion that arises from depression can be mistaken for senility or dementia. At the furthest extreme, thoughts can become incoherent and chaotic. Styron writes of this mental state, "At a later stage, my entire mind would be dominated by anarchic disconnections." Some deeply depressed individuals even experience hallucinations and become delusional.

Anxiety and dread out of proportion to actual events can also occur with depression; indeed, research indicates that more than 60 percent of depressed people feel intense anxiety. My client Paula described her anxiety as profoundly gripping. Her jaw and mouth and the rest of her face were so drawn and tight that she would literally shake while trying to take a sip of water. "I'm afraid of everything," she told me. "It's like being on a runaway train. I'm doing everything I can to slow it down, but I keep missing stop after stop after stop."

BODY

Depressed individuals may experience disruptions in their normal eating and sleep habits. Most lose their appetite, but some actually eat more as a result of the illness, or at times binge and at other times are incapable of eating. Andy, a fifteen-year-old suddenly thrust into the role of being the man in the family, gained thirty pounds over the summer following his parents' separation and his dad's moving away.

Sleep and fatigue are also major issues. Depressed individuals may awaken early, they may be unable to sleep at all, or they may sleep many more hours than usual. Even if they do sleep, it can be a restless, dreamless, uneasy slumber or one wracked with nightmares filled with images of death, devastation, and darkness. Consequently, sleep gives them little relief from their all-encompassing sense of fatigue. Exhaustion is common.

The loss of interest in sex can also accompany depression. For other depressed people, the need for sexual intimacy becomes an insatiable hunger that leads to constant anxiety about abandonment and rejection. Self-loathing and self-devaluing, especially directed toward the inadequacies of one's body, can become the focus of the depression.

BEHAVIOR

Lethargy, an inability to get work done, and difficulty reading or studying are all symptoms of depression. Deep groans may accompany every breath. A client of mine named Jonathan told me in a session, "I heard a funny sound come out of my body, like an owl hooting. But in reality, I was making these heavy, moaning sighs."

Some individuals constantly burst into tears, or are just on the edge of "losing it," crying at any perceived slight. Others seem stooped and shuffling, while still others are agitated and jittery. Some depressed individuals are able to function despite their illness, while others find it impossible to perform simple daily activities like getting dressed, preparing or eating a meal, washing themselves, or going to work.

Unfortunately, these symptoms seem to interact with and reinforce one another. One can lead to another, and they can eventually develop into a downward spiral that becomes increasingly difficult to resolve without treatment.

IS YOUR LOVED ONE DEPRESSED?

On the depression continuum, a more serious condition than the blues is dysthymia, a chronic low-grade melancholy that lasts for at least two years but does not dramatically affect everyday functioning. At the other end of the continuum is major depression, during which one's functioning is impaired. This can be a life-threatening situation; people in the grips of major depression can be actively suicidal.

According to the fourth edition of the *Diagnostic and Statistical Manual of Mental Disorders (DSM-IV-TR,* for short), the psychologist's diagnostic manual, the criteria for diagnosing major depression are that the sufferer has experienced depressed moods for the major part of every day for nearly two weeks, has experienced changes in appetite, sleep, and physical activity, and has suicidal thoughts.

The following checklist can help you determine whether your loved one is depressed and should seek medical and/or therapeutic help:

- Does she feel sad and miserable most of the time?
- Has she lost interest in activities she used to enjoy?
- Has she lost interest in sex?
- Does she seem apathetic or lethargic?
- Are her thoughts, movements, and speech slower than usual?
- Does she become frightened for no apparent reason? Do her fears seem exaggerated?
- Has she suddenly become extremely dependent?
- Does she complain of vague, mysterious physical pain that seems to migrate to different sites around her body?
- Is she able to take care of her physical needs like washing, dressing, eating, and so on? Does it take great effort for her to accomplish simple tasks?
- Does she experience fits of crying or does she feel like crying all the time?
- Does she seem confused or forgetful?
- Does she have difficulty making decisions?
- Does she seem restless and agitated?
- Is she having difficulty sleeping?

- Does she seem exhausted most of the time?
- Does she sleep for hours on end without actually feeling rested?
- Is she unusually irritable?
- Does she express feelings of emptiness and guilt?
- Does she feel helpless and hopeless?
- Has she lost her appetite? Has she lost a significant amount of weight (5 percent of her body weight in a month) without dieting?
- Is she suddenly overeating?
- Does she express feelings of worthlessness and excessive, inappropriate pessimism?
- Does she seem to have a hard time concentrating?
- Does she have repeated thoughts of death and suicide?
- Has she planned or attempted suicide?

If you answer yes to the first two items *and* to any four other items on this list—especially the last question—then chances are good that your loved one is suffering from depression. In Part 2, we'll address what to do if this is the case.

THE CAUSES OF DEPRESSION

Unfortunately, depression is often not attributable to a single factor, but to the interrelation of several predisposing conditions, which can erupt into a full-blown depressive episode given the right—or wrong—mix of life events. Defining the causes of this illness can be a chicken-or-egg proposition.

HEREDITY

Genetics may play a role. Depression or suicidality in a member of one's family seems to increase one's chances for having the illness. Scientists have recently located genetic markers that indicate a susceptibility to manic-depressive illness. Research has also shown that if one identical twin is depressed, the other has a 70 percent chance of being depressed too. And today a great deal of research is taking place, based on the decoded human genome, to determine whether certain genetic patterns can predispose one to depression.

Kate, age thirty-five, expained: "I thought it was just me, but I went home to Detroit for a wedding and the cousins got together and talked about which uncle and whose aunt had been hospitalized or divorced or had committed suicide. After that trip, I realized how much more complicated my depression really was. I always used to say we were a crazy family, but now I *really* knew it!"

The chicken-egg, nurture-versus-nature conundrum here lies in the fact that in a depressed household, there is a strong likelihood that the environment *itself* creates a milieu that is depressing. As you can imagine, if a parent is depressed, home life will be difficult to adjust to—at times even unbearable. Having no place else to go, one could be overwhelmed by feeling trapped. Under such circumstances, it's easy to be drawn into the consequences of familial disruption.

PSYCHOLOGICAL FACTORS

Feeling alone, rejected, or abandoned are the causes and markers of psychological wounds that may predispose an individual to feeling depressed. Many experts point to the early loss or rejecting behavior of a parent as a factor influencing the development of depression. Styron captures the essence of these issues in *Darkness Visible:*

> [A]n even more significant factor was the death of my mother when
> I was thirteen; this disorder and early sorrow—the death or disap-

*pearance of a parent, especially a mother, before or during puberty—
appears repeatedly in the literature on depression as a trauma sometimes likely to create nearly irreparable emotional havoc.*

As Styron explains, a child who has been unable to fully mourn
the loss of a parent can carry within "an insufferable burden of
which rage and guilt, and not only dammed-up sorrow, are a part
and become the potential seeds of self-destruction."

Styron's eloquent description relates well to how neuroscien-
tists are now viewing the impact on the brain of early psychological losses such as the death of a parent, abandonment, or abuse.
There appears to be an interplay between these early traumatic
events and changes in actual brain neurophysiology—the hard-
wiring of the brain. Once the stress of such traumas has altered
neural pathways, subsequent losses—even seemingly small ones—
that remind the individual of the original distress can trigger a full-
blown depressive episode. Peter D. Kramer, an associate clinical
professor of psychiatry at Brown University, theorizes in his
groundbreaking book *Listening to Prozac* that as the illness worsens,
episodes can be triggered independent of apparent precipitating
events.

ENVIRONMENTAL STRESSORS

Job loss, conflictual relationships, retirement, natural disasters,
legal problems, and a death in the family must also be taken into
account as factors in depression. A physical condition can also be
an environmental stressor. The overproduction of certain hormones such as cortisol in response to stressful situations can create
an imbalance in the brain that leads to depression.

One must also bear in mind that, as Drs. John H. Greist and
James W. Jefferson write in *Depression and Its Treatment*, "Depression
can also *cause* impaired relationships, job problems, financial stress—
many of the things that some people feel bring on depression."

Why is it that some individuals respond to stressors such as these by taking charge with resiliency, while others become depressed? Perhaps the ability to tolerate stress is also genetically determined, or perhaps the severity of the stress is the key. Kenneth got the blues after a raging brushfire destroyed his hillside home. After several weeks of grieving, he began picking up the pieces of his life. But an earthquake several months later forced him to shut down his café, exacerbating his sense of panic and grief. As the months went by, he found it difficult to rebuild once more, drifting into a full-blown depression. The additional stress was just too much for him to absorb.

Chronic, long-term illness can also be a stressor that leads to depression. In chapter 9, we will cover this issue in depth.

AN IMBALANCE IN BRAIN CHEMISTRY

That depression seems to run in families indicates that certain individuals have a genetic propensity for these imbalances. Further, that depression in many cases has been so successfully treated with medications that alter the chemistry of the brain and that some people become depressed for no apparent reason suggests that the illness can also be traced to a chemical imbalance in the brain. In true chicken-or-egg fashion, however, it is unclear whether the imbalance causes the pessimistic moods and depressive episodes, or whether these episodes exert such stress on one's system that they disrupt the normal secretion and re-uptake of neurotransmitters within the brain.

Moreover, the symptoms of physical illnesses, such as Parkinson's disease, hypoglycemia, chronic fatigue syndrome, diabetes, renal failure, and others, may include feelings of depression.

Many medications have been linked to depression in some individuals:

- birth control pills
- heart and high blood pressure medications such as beta blockers and calcium channel blockers
- Halcion, Ativan, or other sleeping pills
- cortisone and other steroids
- antibiotics

Alcohol or other substances that might be abused can also contribute to depression. Moderately depressed people, for example, may feel better for twenty or thirty minutes after consuming alcohol. However, the depression will subsequently worsen.

Women can experience symptoms of depression or a cyclical worsening of depressive states owing to premenstrual syndrome. Moreover, the birth of a baby can trigger the "postpartum blues," as hormone levels fall dramatically. For most women the weepiness passes quickly, but for about 10 percent—and especially those who already have a history of depression—the postpartum blues can turn into clinical depression if they persist several weeks after delivery. Fortunately, most postpartum women respond well to psychotherapy and antidepressant medications.

ATYPICAL DEPRESSION

Atypical depression is depression that does not follow all the "rules" and consequently can be difficult to diagnose. Unlike a classically depressed individual, a person with atypical depression may cheer up and feel better when good things happen in her life. She may even enjoy sex and food or other pleasures. Rather than loss of appetite and insomnia, she may experience overeating and oversleeping. Those who have atypical depression seem particularly sensitive to rejection.

According to Elizabeth Wurtzel, author of *Prozac Nation*, "The atypically depressed are more likely to be the walking wounded, people like me who are quite functional, whose lives proceed almost as usual, except that they're depressed all the time, almost constantly embroiled in thoughts of suicide even as they go through their paces."

Wurtzel points out that the depression can be quite severe—even life-threatening—but still allow a semblance of normalcy. If untreated, however, atypical depression can worsen over time. The danger here is that the person who suffers from this illness may commit suicide out of frustration for the disparities in her productive yet gloomy life.

MANIC-DEPRESSIVE ILLNESS

Individuals with manic-depressive illness, also called bipolar disorder, swing from the lows of depression that I've described in these pages to exaggerated highs. At first the manic phases may be mild; in this phase, individuals suffering from manic-depressive illness may feel powerful, full of energy, giddy with excitement, seductive, bubbly, elated, euphoric . . . in short, pretty wonderful. These *hypomanic* phases, as they are called, can, however, devolve into much more intense activity in which life seems to spin out of control. Their friends may complain, "Slow down, I can't keep up with you." During a manic episode, manic-depressives may

- talk too fast, too loud, and without stopping, moving from one idea to the next in rapid succession, but not necessarily logically
- move too fast
- stop sleeping and eating altogether
- act self-confident and grandiose even when the situation doesn't warrant it

- begin many projects at once without the wherewithal to complete them
- buy impulsively and excessively or otherwise use poor judgment such as driving recklessly
- engage in promiscuity or unusual sexual behavior
- become impatient, irritable, agitated, volatile, violent, and even psychotic when thwarted

These manic episodes are invariably followed by deep depressions of the kind outlined earlier. When bipolar illness is not treated or is undertreated, it can lead to a much more debilitating condition called rapid cycling manic depression. This condition is marked by frequent mood changes from one day to the next, and even from hour to hour.

WHEN DOES DEPRESSION STRIKE?

Depression can occur at any time in one's life, though it becomes more common as we age.

DEPRESSION IN CHILDREN

We may be unused to thinking about depression occurring in young children, but there is a growing body of evidence that it does. Mental health surveys have found that one in fifty elementary school children suffers from depression that would benefit from treatment.

In some children, the typical symptoms of depression may be:

- aggressiveness toward people, animals, or property
- disruptive classroom behavior and/or changes in school performance
- tantrums

- anxiety, especially about separating from parents
- many physical complaints without a detectable cause
- various learning disabilities (especially the impulsiveness and distractability associated with Attention Deficit Disorder [ADD])

Other depressed youngsters may refuse to play with their friends, have a persistently sad demeanor, seem slowed in their speech and movements, and withdraw from social interaction.

Research has shown that depression can have its roots in early life. In fact, today it is considered a developmental disorder—it can begin during childhood. One study of youngsters who became severely depressed as adolescents demonstrated that they shared certain behavioral traits as younger children: depressed teenage boys had been impulsive, unsocialized, and aggressive, and depressed girls had been fearful, shy, overly concerned about the acceptability of their behavior, and introspective. Children who are unpopular because of their hostility or shyness and those with low self-esteem who are unduly harsh in their self-criticism are also at greater risk for depression.

Seeking therapy for a depression-prone child at an early age can help avert more severe depressive episodes as the youngster faces the challenges of adolescence.

DEPRESSION IN ADOLESCENTS

For several years, I taught a course for professionals at U.C.L.A. Extension entitled "The Angry Adolescent: The Sheep in Wolf's Clothing," dealing with misperceptions and misinterpretations of adolescent behavior. What I had found in doing preparatory research for this course was that although episodes of anger during adolescence seem to be typical, persistent anger is a cry for help and can be a sign of depression.

Depression in adolescents may be cloaked in "normal" if not

predictable teenage behavior. Statements such as "But you just don't understand" are seen as normal complaints from a teen to her parent. But when such complaints and behavior are taken to the extreme and become destructive acts, when teens punch fists through walls, destroy computer equipment, or are involved in frequent car accidents, when a night out with friends turns into a two A.M. telephone call informing you that your child has passed out because she drank too much, it can be a sign of depression.

Teens who are depressed may express a strong desire to leave home; they may believe that no one understands them; they may seem restless, grouchy, and aggressive. Some teenagers become sulky, refusing to participate in family activities. They remain holed up in their rooms, listening to music. Others may experience difficulties in school, losing interest in subjects they formerly enjoyed, cutting classes, and not completing homework assignments.

Mary came to see me about her depressed teenage daughter. Angie's poetry writing—a talent of which Mary was proud—had now taken a dark and sinister turn. "She writes with such frightening imagery," this mother lamented, "I'm worried about what's going on in her mind."

Still other teens exhibit true antisocial behavior, using drugs and alcohol and acting out by stealing or becoming involved in street gangs or other violent behavior.

Some depressed teenagers stop caring about their appearance (and seemingly fit right in with grunge chic), while others are oversensitive to loss and rejection in love relationships.

Because so many of these behaviors in a less extreme form can be thought of as signs of typical teenage angst, the depression can be easily missed until the youngster makes a highly dramatic and attention-grabbing gesture such as a suicide attempt. Consequently, it's important to pay attention to these symptoms in teens. Research has shown that depression and manic-depressive illnesses often first manifest themselves during adolescence and early adulthood.

DEPRESSION IN THE ELDERLY

Depression among the elderly is a large and growing problem. It is estimated that one person in seven over the age of 65 suffers from depression. Sadly, only 10–30 percent of these individuals seek treatment.

This may be true in part because depression is difficult to diagnose at this phase of life. Depression in the elderly may be marked by confusion, disorientation, loss of memory, difficulty concentrating, inattentiveness, and distractibility. Older people may seem apathetic, no longer enjoying activities that once gave them pleasure or tending to their personal hygiene.

Unfortunately, these symptoms mimic dementia or Alzheimer's disease, and it's easy for a depressed older person to be misdiagnosed. Harry, a sixty-eight-year-old retiree, had not made a smooth transition to his new nonworking status. He seemed confused and withdrawn and could barely concentrate long enough to read the newspaper. His wife and son thought that he was depressed about having been "downsized" out of his career. After several months, he began losing things and accusing his wife of hiding them. After a series of discussions with a neurologist, the physician diagnosed Alzheimer's. Harry's low mood was a by-product of the condition.

According to some experts, to tell the difference between Alzheimer's disease and depression, it helps to ask questions eliciting information, such as "What is your date of birth?" or "What is your address?" Depressed individuals may take a stab at answering the question, and perhaps halt in the middle, confessing they've forgotten or don't know the answer, but those with Alzheimer's will give a grossly inappropriate answer, such as an address when asked their date of birth.

In addition, brain injuries and strokes can lead to psychiatric problems such as depression. Again, careful analysis and diagnosis are necessary to pinpoint the true origin of the individual's behavior and moods.

❖

If after reading this chapter you are convinced that your loved one is depressed, take heart. This recognition is an important first step in getting help. Information, facts, and real-life stories are the beginning of tracking the course of the disease. As we'll discuss in later chapters, how you present this information to your loved one is integral to how he or she gets help.

◆

CHAPTER 3

The Impact of Your Loved One's Depression on You

Dᴜʀɪɴɢ ᴍʏ ᴍᴏᴛʜᴇʀ'ꜱ ᴅᴀʀᴋᴇꜱᴛ ᴛɪᴍᴇꜱ, ɪᴛ ᴡᴀꜱ ᴀꜱ if I had disappeared. I remember going unnoticed—being invisible. No one asked, "What is happening to Mitch? Why is he so angry? Why is he doing so poorly in school?" No one, that is, except Mr. Scott, my high school physics teacher, and his attention came at quite a cost.

One afternoon when I was in twelfth grade, Mr. Scott abandoned his lecture on velocity and mass to devote the entire hour to a discussion of integrity, trust, and values. He had spent some years in Africa teaching in the Peace Corps, and on this day he claimed that he had never, in all his varied experiences as an instructor, encountered such a blatant disregard for honesty as he had on the part of one student in one of his classes.

At the end of the period, before dismissing us, he stood up and, to my horror, called me into his office. It was obvious to everyone that I was that person he had spoken about with such vehemence. I felt devastated.

My offense? Mr. Scott had found my crib notes inadvertently shuffled into the pages of a makeup exam that I had taken after an absence of several days. Of course, he had no idea that my "illness" was due to my mother's problems. And he couldn't have known that I was incapable of concentrating on any of my assignments, let alone applying what I didn't understand in trigonometry to what I was supposed to be learning in physics. In desperation, I had asked a friend to give me the questions and go over the answers, hoping Mr. Scott wouldn't bother creating a new exam just for me. At the time, I didn't have a clue how else to help myself.

When my teacher confronted me with the evidence of my cheating, I began to shake. This had never happened before. Until now, I had been a completely trustworthy though, of late, underachieving pupil.

Mr. Scott remembered me from ninth grade as an A student in his physical science class. Between attempting to make me feel as guilty as possible and deciding what he was going to do with me, he muttered casually under his breath—as if in an afterthought—"Mitch, what happened between *then* and *now*?" And then he just stared at me, waiting for a reply.

I started to cry, as much as a graduating, football-playing high school senior could cry—my lip quivering and my eyes burning and red. I tried to stay away from his comment in my response, but his words kept burrowing into my thoughts. "What happened between *then* and *now*?" What had happened . . . Even to me, my home life seemed completely unrelated to my inappropriate behavior. It had never occurred to me that the two could be linked or that I was feeling so desperate because of the impact of my mom's condition on me.

I was deeply confused and troubled. Unable to find a coherent answer, I was only capable of whispering, "I'm sorry. It won't happen again."

Somehow in all the turmoil, Mr. Scott gave me another chance. I believe he felt sorry for me. But, although I was off the hook, I felt ashamed long after the incident faded from everyone else's memory.

Ironically, for years afterward Mr. Scott was my favorite teacher: Finally someone had paid attention to me—had taken what happened seriously and had spoken with passion. At the time, it didn't matter that it came as a result of my having cheated . . . at my emotional expense.

I think back on those years and realize that I had sacrificed my integrity just trying to survive. Today, I clutch the preservation of my integrity as a way of keeping at bay the memories of those times and the possibility of their return. Losing integrity tears at your soul. It's like being set adrift on the high seas without a compass or map linking you to the shore.

I think back to that time and tenderly understand that what I needed then was a safe harbor. A place where I could just float and feel comfortable and at ease. A place where I wouldn't have to speak, but would be understood. I found none.

Indeed, listening every night to my mother's ranting mixed with her terrible sorrow, I learned, instead, how much a soul can absorb of another's pain, and it broke my heart.

BURDENS YOU MAY BE FACING

When I was older, my encounter with Mr. Scott stood out as a marker. Until then, I had been quite blind to the profound changes that had occurred within me as a result of my mother's illness—my difficulties keeping up with a normal workload, my feelings of guilt and shame coupled with an unconscious need for secrecy, my willingness to compromise my integrity just to get by, my loneliness, my desperation, my anger. Later, my psychologist mind wondered whether my leaving those crib notes behind was an unconscious cry for help. Perhaps it was.

You may find yourself similarly affected. Depression can take a terrible toll on the individual afflicted with this illness, but it can also have an intense impact on you. And this can be particularly true today, with the huge changes in the health-care system limiting or curtailing treatment or hospitalization, thereby multiplying and intensifying families' caregiving responsibilities.

Many scientific studies have investigated the burdens that family and friends of depressed individuals bear, and their findings are consistent: The depression of someone you love can influence your work life and financial status, your emotions, your relationship with your loved one, and your sense of control over your life. It can make you feel stigmatized and alone and can raise your anxiety level.

The authors of one such study, Miriam Jacob and her colleagues at the University of Pittsburgh School of Medicine, quote the husband of a thirty-seven-year-old woman who suffered from recurrent depression:

> *I have always felt like I was walking on eggs, but no matter how softly I walked, they broke. . . . I often thought, "I don't know this person." When you are constantly being the provider and not receiving support and comfort, you become very discouraged. . . . Eventually, I felt lost and unsuccessful.*

This man's reactions to his wife's symptoms are all too familiar. This withdrawal and compassion fatigue—reaching the limit of one's ability to be understanding—can be dangerous. The degree of burden and distress that you experience when relating to your depressed loved one can affect the support and acceptance you provide her. The more you can bring to your conscious awareness your unexpressed feelings and concerns, the more you can begin to help both of you.

The following questions, gleaned from the many research questionnaires developed for caregivers, are meant to encourage you to bring to consciousness the impact that your loved one's depression has on you. This understanding is the first step in your finding a way to help yourself and your loved one.

- Have you had to make any adjustments in your life (such as changing your work schedule or cutting back on social activities) in order to cope with the depression? If so, what kinds of changes?
- Have household routines such as mealtimes or bedtimes been upset?
- Have you suffered financial reverses because of the illness?
- How did you feel when you discovered that your loved one was suffering from depression? Sad? Frightened? Upset? Guilty? Embarrassed? Relieved?
- How do you feel about it right now?
- Do you feel that your loved one is a different person since the onset of the illness?
- Do you behave differently now around your loved one? Are you "walking on eggs"?
- If your loved one has bipolar illness, how have the manic phases manifested themselves? How has that affected you?
- Does anyone else know about how you are feeling?
- Has the depression created friction in your relationship with your loved one? If so, how?
- Do you feel you have neglected other family members because of the depression?

- Do you feel as if your life is spinning out of control?
- Do you feel trapped or resentful?
- Has your productivity at work been impacted?
- Have your co-workers commented, "You don't seem yourself lately"?
- Do people minimize your problems?
- Do you resent that your loved one has become more dependent on you?
- Do you fear that your behavior might worsen the situation?
- Do you find yourself worrying about the future a lot?
- Do you feel angry?
- Have you found it difficult to concentrate on your own activities?
- Do you sometimes wish you could run away from the problem?
- Do you sometimes feel hopeless and depressed yourself?

If, after reviewing these questions, you find that your loved one's depression has made a surprisingly significant impact on your life, rest assured that most people in your situation struggle with similar issues. It is normal and to be expected for you to experience some anxiety and difficulty when someone you love is depressed. In Part 2, you will find many suggestions to help you cope with the impact the depression may be having on your life.

For now, while keeping your answers to these preliminary questions in mind, let's look more closely at some of the thorny issues they raise.

THE IMPACT ON YOUR WORK LIFE AND FINANCIAL STATUS

The most immediately measurable and concrete impact of your loved one's depression—especially if you are the spouse or the parents—can be a financial one. The cost of hospitalization and ongoing psychotherapy and medication can be formidable, particularly if your loved one is uninsured or underinsured.

If the depressed individual is a family breadwinner and can no longer work consistently, or if she is a dependent whose condition requires constant supervision (or both!), you are likely to be financially strapped.

Some depressed individuals—most notably those who are manic-depressive—handle money poorly and may spend lavishly and impulsively when in a manic phase, leaving the family with huge debts.

A family friend whose sister was diagnosed as manic-depressive when in her twenties some twenty-five years ago told me how the illness impacted her parents' financial stability. "My parents depleted their savings trying to help my sister," Mimi said. "Initially they put Lisa in a posh private hospital populated with the bored alcoholic sons and daughters of Connecticut's rich, landed gentry. The doctors doped her up on lithium, which enveloped her in a disturbing haze. . . . Four weeks and eight thousand dollars later, my parents brought her home again. She seemed to be better but then she experienced an adverse reaction to the lithium . . . and could no longer take the medication. . . .

"Always my parents searched for another psychiatrist, another medication, another *anything* that would ease my sister's terrible torment. . . . It was a cycle that repeated itself over and over for years—fancy institutions, new therapies, new drugs. . . . At a time when most people were looking forward to retirement, to a well-deserved rest after a lifetime of toil, my father was still working to pay Lisa's medical bills."

Sadly, Mimi's story is not atypical. In Chapter 11, I will discuss strategies to help you navigate the health-care system and diminish some of those burdens. For now, it's important to keep in mind that the financial pressure can deeply affect you and your loved one.

THE IMPACT ON YOUR EMOTIONS

Researchers have associated many, many emotions with having a depressed loved one. These can include

- fear, anxiety, and worry
- frustration and anger
- grief
- a sense of burden or being overwhelmed
- shame
- guilt
- annoyance
- resentment
- embarrassment
- entrapment
- feeling neglected
- hopelessness and discouragement
- depression

When someone you love is depressed, you may live with a chronic sense of uncertainty, never really knowing when your loved one will recover from a depressive episode or fall into a new one. You can feel profound loss—even grief and anger—that life has deviated, maybe permanently, from the norm.

Research by Georgene Eakes, a professor of psychiatric mental health nursing at the School of Nursing at East Carolina University in Greenville, North Carolina, indicates that parents of mentally ill adult children live with "chronic sorrow" intertwined with anger and frustration.

"It's important to note," Eakes wrote in an article published in *Archives of Psychiatric Nursing,* "that feelings of anger permeated the experience of chronic sorrow for these parents of mentally ill adult children. . . . The unending caregiving associated with being the parent of a mentally ill child was the most common trigger of chronic sorrow. . . . Parents reported feeling a never-ending sense of responsibility for their child which at times was overwhelming."

It is important to express your feelings, whatever they may be. Research has indicated that repressing and/or suppressing your emotions rather than addressing them does more harm than good to you and your loved one. Holding back can put you at greater risk for cardiac disease, cancer, an impaired immune response, gastrointestinal complaints, and stress-related headaches.

In contrast, writing or talking about the traumas you have experienced and your reactions to your loved one's situation can enhance your physical and mental health. In Chapter 4, you will find some appropriate ways to deal with the emotional impact of your loved one's depression on you.

THE IMPACT ON YOUR RELATIONSHIP

Depression can put a great deal of strain on your relationship with your loved one. The illness can itself make relating difficult.

In a study of recurrent depression and its effect on family burden and attitudes, Miriam Jacob and her colleagues found that family members living with depressed individuals had a harder time coping with their loved one's symptoms than those living apart. No matter what the living arrangements, however, all family members found it most upsetting to hear their loved ones express feelings of worthlessness, inadequacy, and low self-esteem. Apathy and disinterest in usual activities were also distressing to family members, as were the depressed individual's constant ruminations, worrying, and low moods.

Your Spouse

If the depressed person is your spouse or significant other, the illness can create disturbances within your relationship. Interactions may be characterized by a new unwelcome dependency, the breakdown of communication, tension, and resentment.

Steve and Andrea, a couple I was counseling, became mired in their confusing and difficult emotions. Andrea had been depressed for some time. She was highly sensitive to rejection and would react to any perceived slight with rage. Steve, for his part, became angry at Andrea's volatility. "She's biting the hand that's supporting her," he griped. But their problems didn't stop there.

When Andrea came home from work complaining about her tyrannical boss, Steve, in his attempts to soothe his wife, would share his own difficulties in dealing with a critical supervisor. "You're always turning the conversation back on yourself," Andrea would cry. "Don't you care about what's happening with me?"

At this Steve would feel hurt that his attempts to help were being rebuffed and even attacked. From his point of view, he was offering support the only way he knew how. And so he would angrily return the volley: "What do you mean I don't care about you? Oh, why bother talking to you anyway? I can never get through." And on it went.

Recriminations such as these left this couple feeling as if they were both angry, depressed, alone, misunderstood, and rejected. They blamed each other for their unhappiness. After a while, it became unclear which one had the problem and what the cause of that problem was. We had to work hard to establish boundaries and put the emotions in the marriage back on a more even keel.

The depression can not only disrupt your relationship but also inhibit your spouse from fulfilling his or her expected role within the family—to work outside the home, care for the children, carry out household chores, prepare meals, organize family finances, and so on. Intimacy and sexuality may come to a grinding halt, or there may be a greater dependency and a suffocating need for intimacy. Family activities that you once shared may suddenly fall squarely on your shoulders alone. There can be a loss of companionship and a collapse in communication. These and other disruptions in the course of family life can create resentment and tension.

As you can imagine, this kind of friction can prolong a depressive episode or even contribute to the onset of a new one.

Your Child

As I noted above, the parent-child relationship can be marked with sorrow and anger when the child is suffering from depression. Mental illnesses often first make their appearance during late adolescence—a time when parents and children are naturally separating—and the depression at this age can disrupt a normal stage of development. Like it or not, the depressed teen finds himself thrown back into a more dependent position, which can exacerbate family tensions.

As with our friend Mimi's parents, the care and supervision of a depressed child can trouble parents for the rest of their lives. They may fear he will never get better or that he may need constant supervision. They wonder whether treatments will work. Research has shown that the two most common concerns of parents of depressed children are the following:

- GUILT: What did I do to cause this terrible illness?
- LONG-TERM CARE: Who will care for our child when we're gone?

Parents often view child rearing as a lifetime project in which they involve themselves with great hope, no matter what their child's age or status. Mental illness and chronic depression can create a sense of "project loss" for parents. They worry whether their child will be able to succeed in life, to graduate from school, to find a job and become independent, to have a home and family of his own. They look for signs to affirm that he's really O.K. This may seem like denial, but it often grows out of the desire and hope that the person they remember will return.

Parents of depressed children may worry about what the future holds in store, or, as one of my patients plaintively asked in reference to her depressed son, "Is there a future in our future?"

Your Brother or Sister

If your sibling is depressed, you may worry that the illness will strike you as well—or, paradoxically, you may feel guilty that it has not. Don felt anxious and resentful about taking charge of caring for his sister who suffered from bipolar illness when his parents could no longer carry that burden as they aged. Others feel the full brunt of their sibling's illness when their parents pass away.

You may feel upset that the family's attention and money seem to flow mostly in the direction of your ill sibling, and you may feel as disturbed as other members of your family about your loved one's behavior and attitude. You may even develop your own set of physical symptoms—headaches or upset stomach—or you may feel that you shouldn't complain and burden your parents even more than they already are burdened.

Your Parents

Young children whose mothers and/or fathers are depressed may suffer from serious health and behavior problems. According to an investigation at the Yale University School of Medicine carried out by Myrna M. Weissman and Karen John and their research team in the departments of psychiatry and epidemiology, these youngsters are themselves at risk for depression, anxiety disorders, and other disturbances including learning disabilities, behavioral problems, accident-prone behavior, and a higher incidence of hospitalization. Children of depressed parents make significantly more suicide attempts than children whose parents are not depressed.

When I was reading this research, I suddenly stopped in midsentence. I remembered having four car accidents between October of my senior year in high school—the same period as the physics cheating incident—and the first year of college. Now I can guess that at least part of the cause of those accidents was my feeling distracted by my mother's illness. At the time, however, I blamed myself.

Other researchers have suggested that the emotional unavailability and irritability of depressed mothers may produce distressed, insecure children. These youngsters can be at greater risk for low self-esteem. They may lack the energy to engage in intellectual, physical, or social activities that enhance their development. Or, as Peter D. Kramer makes clear in *Listening to Prozac,* a depressed mother's child becomes highly attuned to his mother's emotional states, carefully observing every nuance and change. "In adult life," he writes, "some [of these grown-up children] maintain a compulsive need to please and are thought to have a knack for behaving just as friends (or therapists) prefer, at whatever cost to themselves."

In addition, children might feel guilty that they were somehow responsible for their depressed parents' illness. Sometimes, a depressed parent's behavior can reinforce this feeling. One of my patients, Kim, described how her father would lash out at her when in one of his sullen moods. "He would erupt and blame me in a global way for everything that was wrong," Kim said. "He pointed to the dirty kitchen or to my room being a mess as proof of my guilt. I remember desperately rushing to put things right in order to placate him and assuage my guilt. But it didn't help."

Of course, adult children of depressed parents are also impacted by the illness. I found myself distracted from my own life whenever my mother experienced another depressive episode—and they continued fairly frequently throughout her life. The thoughts I had had as a teenager would intrude into my adult life, but now I had bigger responsibilities: a family, job, continued schooling. I had to find a way to limit how much responsibility I would take for her care. It was a matter of survival for me.

As the adult child of a depressed parent, you must contend with issues of boundaries and autonomy. How involved can you be? How much control should you take of your parent's life?

Claudia had spent months struggling with her severely depressed elderly mother, Martha, whose condition had been triggered by her husband's sudden death. Martha had tried various medications and therapy, but hers was one of those unusually resistant cases and none of these remedies worked. After nearly a year of her mother's treatments, as a last resort Claudia gave up her part-time job and moved Martha into her home to care for her. For several more months Claudia devoted her life to her mom, but there were still minimal results.

Claudia could no longer go on like this. Finally, after discussion with her mother's psychiatrist, she decided that hospitalization was the only answer. After a series of electroconvulsive therapy treatments (see Chapter 8), Martha snapped out of her despondency and began to enjoy her life again. Claudia, having realized that she had reached her limit, helped save her mother's life.

When caring for a depressed parent, it is also helpful to communicate with friends and family members to divide the responsibilities.

Your Friend

When a friend has the blues or is seriously depressed, you may feel helpless, as if you're on the outside. You may want to step in but fear that you're intruding. Or you may learn that your friend has confided in you about his depression but has kept it from his family.

It is burdensome to keep such a secret, especially if you fear that your friend may be suicidal. In this case, it would be wise to alert family members and other friends. Involve as many people as you can.

LOSS OF CONTROL

When facing a chronic illness, most individuals and their families feel as if their lives have spun out of their control. Former first lady Rosalynn Carter remarked in her book, *Helping Yourself Help Others,* "You may feel as if your life's course is now dictated by the whims of your dependent one's illness. This is truly frightening."

The situation is no different when someone you love is depressed. You may find it difficult to plan from day to day, week to week, or year to year. So much can be riding on your loved one's condition at any given moment.

Interestingly, research has found that the greater your sense of control, the less burdened you will feel by your loved one's illness. In Chapter 4, you'll find ways to feel more in charge of your life at this difficult time.

STIGMATIZATION

Unfortunately, there is still a stigma—a very negative perception—attached to mental illnesses such as depression and manic depression. In a survey the National Alliance for the Mentally Ill (NAMI) found:

- Seventy-one percent of respondents think that mental illness is due to emotional weakness.
- Sixty-five percent say that bad parenting is at fault; 35 percent think it's due to sinful behavior.
- Only 10 percent know that severe mental illness has a biological basis and involves the brain.

Unfortunately, research has shown that the more caregivers believe a mental illness is stigmatized, the more burdened they will feel. This stigma can be exacerbated when others, in the guise of wanting to be helpful toward the depressed person, blame you for your loved one's problems. One patient described a scene at a party that felt terrible to her. When Janice walked into the kitchen to join the conversation, the entire roomful of people fell silent. She later learned that the crowd had been talking about her problems—not the problems she was having struggling with dealing with her depressed husband but what *she* wasn't doing, and worse yet, how she was contributing to Hal's moods.

"I can't believe these are my friends," she complained bitterly. "How could they be so judgmental and insensitive? Don't they know about all the doctor's visits, and second opinions, and the emergency phone calls to the hospital? Don't they see that I'm working overtime and on weekends to supplement our lost income and pay for some of the huge medical expenses we're facing?"

Another phenomenon is that out of discomfort, other people may refrain from asking questions about your depressed loved one. They may act as if he doesn't exist, or they may discourage you from talking about the illness and its impact on you. They may make kidding or insensitive comments about your loved one's "craziness."

Taken together, these reactions can leave you feeling blamed and ashamed and even more isolated.

Perhaps the unspoken messages of stigma and secrecy that I had picked up in my family were at the root of my unwillingness to discuss with my physics teacher why I was doing so poorly in school. Perhaps I was too embarrassed to talk about my mother's state.

ISOLATION

You may find yourself feeling very alone with your situation. If, as in Janice's case, friends or other family members criticize your way of dealing with your loved one; if they're unwilling to help in ways that would be meaningful to you or only grudgingly offer assistance; if they only seem to make the situation worse; if they withdraw from you or your loved one or foist unwanted or erroneous advice on you, you may feel isolated with your problems.

Friends, not knowing what to do or how to behave, may feel uncomfortable and withdraw from a depressed individual—and from you, if you are living in the same household. Or you may be afraid to leave your loved one alone, for fear of what he might do in your absence, thereby cutting yourself off from your own social network. You may also believe that no one fully understands what you're going through.

If your depressed loved one is your spouse or someone whose companionship you enjoyed, you can miss his company—the friend you used to laugh and play with—because of his intense need to withdraw.

Moreover, as Rosalynn Carter points out in *Helping Yourself Help Others,* "When caregivers perceive themselves as being alone and in 'second place' with no one to talk to or help out, they often feel trapped—literally imprisoned in their own households. These feelings can lead to intense anger and depression, which can further drive away friends and family."

Unwanted aloneness creates enormous stress in our lives. In Chapter 4, I'll provide some suggestions for dealing with this difficult consequence of depression.

ANXIETY

When you consider the impact of your loved one's depression on your financial picture, your emotions, your relationship, your sense of control, your feeling stigmatized, and your isolation, is it any wonder that your anxiety might increase? Add to that the unpredictability of the course of the illness, and you can see why the depression can be enormously stressful to you.

FACTORS THAT CAN INFLUENCE
AND LESSEN THE IMPACT

As I explained earlier in the chapter, the degree of burden and distress that you experience when relating to your depressed loved one can affect the support and acceptance you provide him. That's why it will be important for everyone's benefit that you lessen, in whatever way you can, the impact of a loved one's depression on you.

You should know that there are factors that can mitigate the distress you feel. These include

- your ongoing relationship with your loved one
- support you receive from other members of your family, support networks and self-help groups, the community, and/or mental health providers
- your own coping strategies
- information about the course of the illness
- other life events that can render your life more pleasant

Let's move on now to the many steps you can take to help you deal with your loved one's illness.

PART II

What to Do

◆

CHAPTER 4

Your Role as Strengthened Ally

FOR MANY YEARS, I FACILITATED THERAPEUTIC GROUPS for cancer patients and their families at The Wellness Community in Santa Monica, California. The Wellness Community is an international non-profit organization dedicated to providing free support, education, and hope to people with cancer and their loved ones.

Discussions in the family groups often focused on how family members could help their loved ones with cancer fight for recovery without becoming overwhelmed themselves by the burdens of caregiving. I remember Sylvia, a woman of about fifty-five whose husband had cancer, who talked about how she went about becoming what she called a "strengthened ally."

"Once a week, I make it a point to go out for lunch with my friends," Sylvia confided. "And I make sure to see our granddaughter every Friday. I also visit our son in graduate school as often as I can. When I come back from these outings, I feel refreshed and renewed, And that's when I can be a source of comfort and support to Bill. I'm happy to just hold him, if that's what he needs."

Of course, Sylvia's participation in a peer support group at The Wellness Community—being with others who shared her plight—was also a source of strength and revitalization for her.

I believe that you can use Sylvia's strategies in your role as caregiver and friend to someone who is depressed. Unless you take good care of yourself, you won't be at your most effective when it comes to caring for your loved one. In fact, I have found that individuals who ignore their own needs and self-care for the sake of their ill loved one can eventually experience compassion fatigue and burnout. And that situation can undermine your best efforts to help your loved one deal with her illness.

BURNOUT

Burnout, also called compassion fatigue, is the feeling of having reached the limits of your endurance and your ability to cope. Rosalynn Carter explains in *Helping Yourself Help Others* that burnout results from the combination of your emotional dilemmas (including feelings of helplessness, guilt, and lack of recognition for your efforts), family discord, and isolation. "Add to that the urgency and tension caused by too many demands on one's strength, resources, time, and energy," she writes, "and you can see why many caregivers experience this sense of utter depletion."

Unfortunately, burnout is a common occurrence among caregivers, whether their loved one is suffering from a physical or mental illness. In a study of 175 family caregivers in southwest Georgia, the Rosalynn Carter Institute found that about half of those surveyed believed they were probably suffering from burnout, and 85 percent complained of feeling "just plain exhausted" at the end of the day.

According to the clinical psychologist and burnout expert Dr. Herbert J. Freudenberger, you can recognize that you're suffering from burnout if you experience physical symptoms such as

- headaches
- insomnia
- backaches
- lethargy
- lingering colds
- gastrointestinal upsets
- cardiovascular problems

Burnout also has emotional components. You may find yourself

- frustrated and angry
- empty or sad
- confused and inefficient
- pessimistic
- resentful
- insecure
- disinterested and apathetic
- depressed

These are all expectable reactions to feeling stressed beyond your ability to cope.

Burnout can be emotionally damaging to you and your loved one. Some individuals who feel overwhelmed by the burdens of caring for someone who is depressed may, like my father, seek to escape into their work or hobbies, leaving the depressed individual all the more alone. They may even literally run away. Others may turn to alcohol or drugs to assuage their pain, or they may isolate themselves from their friends, feeling that no one can truly understand their problems. This creates a downward spiral for the whole family.

Clearly, before you can begin to be helpful for your loved one, you will need to know how to cope with the stress of your situation, so that you can avoid burnout. Let's look at some actions you can take to become a strengthened ally. These will enhance your capacity to help your loved one.

BECOMING A STRENGTHENED ALLY

There are many strategies you can take to revitalize your energy. The following suggestions will help you avoid burnout and be more available to your depressed loved one.

1. Get support for yourself. Research has documented that talking to people who share your problems reduces stress and alleviates your sense of isolation. It can feel great to laugh and cry with others who have walked in your shoes. Moreover, those who have covered the same ground before you can offer a wealth of useful suggestions as well as hope for the future. Being involved in a peer support group can lessen the stigma attached to depression.

I see this every day at The Wellness Community, but the value of groups was brought home to me once again in a Dr. Joyce Brothers column. A woman wrote to Dr. Brothers explaining that her husband had been involved in a serious car accident in which a person riding in the other vehicle was killed. Although the other passengers agreed that he was not at fault, this man could not stop blaming himself and became quite depressed, withdrawing and refusing to discuss the incident.

After becoming involved in therapy and beginning to air his feelings, he decided to join a support group. "The results have been amazing," the woman wrote. "It is such a comfort to hear the words you have been feeling for so long coming from another's mouth. It is such a comfort to know that you are not alone."

The National Alliance for the Mentally Ill (NAMI) offers groups for families of those suffering from mental illness. If your loved one has been hospitalized because of the depression, the institution often provides therapeutic groups for family members. Strongly consider attending such a group, even if you commit to only a month to start with—just to see whether the benefits of support outweigh the anxiety you may feel in talking in a group.

In Appendix 2, you will find NAMI's address as well as a list of other organizations that can be helpful to you.

2. *Educate yourself.* Information is empowerment. Understanding the course of depression, the possibility of relapse, the recommended treatments, the side effects of medications, and all the other complexities of this illness can help you anticipate and plan for the future. It will also reduce your feelings of helplessness and prepare you in advance to deal with crises.

In Part 1 of this book, I have provided a brief description of depression and its effects on the individual and his or her family. You might seek out additional, specific information from the professional who is treating your loved one as well as from other books and organizations (see Appendix 1 and Appendix 2).

Keep in mind that you should educate yourself to the degree that you feel comfortable. You needn't become encyclopedic in your knowledge to be well informed or helpful. In fact, sometimes being overly involved in gathering information can be overwhelming and preoccupying. It can even distract you from other ways of nurturing yourself.

3. Keep a journal. Dr. Freudenberger suggests that you keep a "burnout log" to document daily events that create stress in your life. After several weeks you'll be able to identify and then draw some conclusions about hot-button issues for you. Then you can come up with some solutions. For example, perhaps keeping this journal will lead you to realize that you need to allow time for taking a brisk walk or reading an exciting novel if you're feeling particularly oppressed by your loved one's persistently pessimistic attitude.

A journal is also a useful place to dialogue with yourself. You can give yourself positive reinforcement for doing the best you can in a difficult situation. You can vent all the rage and frustration you feel without damaging your relationship with your loved one or other family members. You can brainstorm creative solutions to problems that at first seem unresolvable.

Carole kept such a journal. She brought it to one of her sessions. One entry began with a laundry list of all the things she had to do—work, pick up the children, reorder Josh's medication, prepare his favorite dinner, and so on.

"It really helped me to write that list," she told me. "I realize what a source of comfort I am to Josh. Who would have thought that I could have done so much? It was exciting to check off the items as I did them. In that instant, I could see each chore as a medal of honor, not as a brick on my back."

In addition, keeping a journal can be a stress-reducer and health-enhancer. Research among college students has shown that those who wrote about their feelings in a journal visited the student health center less frequently than their peers who did not keep a journal. Just the act of writing about their emotions helped these students remain healthier.

4. Maintain friendships. Sylvia's strategy of continuing her weekly lunches with her friends and family despite her husband's illness is instructive. Even though you may be feeling miserable, it's important not to isolate yourself from those who may provide support or just distraction. Studies have shown that those who have friends live longer than those who don't!

5. Preserve routines. Often, when someone you love is depressed you feel out of control. The course of the illness, the mood swings, the unpredictability of it all can wreak havoc on your sense of stability. Of course, none of us are in control of everything, but it can be comforting and reassuring to retain and maintain as much control over the routines of life as is reasonable.

For instance, Sylvia decided to have dinner at six P.M. each evening, go to church every Sunday, and to watch her favorite TV shows every Thursday night. These were all simple ways of maintaining a sense of control. Daily routines can create structure and a feeling of safety.

6. Continue with hobbies. By the same token, don't abandon hobbies and other activities that have always given you pleasure. You need to feed your soul in order to be available to your loved one. By continuing to participate in activities that you enjoy, you will have more energy to bring to the relationship. We all need moments to ourselves to replenish our inner reserves. Don't deny yourself this important source of nourishment.

7. Remember that life goes on. Even though your loved one may be suffering, it's wise to remember that you are a separate person and are entitled to enjoy your own life. Attend classes that enhance your growth, start a hobby, go to a movie, make new friends. Don't forsake your life. It has value outside your loved one's depression.

8. Learn to let go. So often, when caregivers are asked how they're doing, they will automatically say, "Oh, I'm fine. Don't worry about me." But that can belie reality. You also need to receive care and concern. The truth is, you can't do it all.

Letting go is a state of mind that helps you become receptive to others' expressions of love and concern. It encompasses being open to the smallest pleasures of life—a bird singing, the warm sun on your back, the scent of a fragrant rose.

Sometimes it's helpful to be passive and just take in what is available around you. Allow yourself to feel replenished from others' gestures—a card, a kind word left on your answering machine, a pat on the arm. Listening to music you enjoy, attending religious services, or watching a video of a favorite movie can also help you recharge your batteries.

Learning to let go is an important step toward avoiding taking on undue responsibility—a topic I'll discuss at greater length below.

9. Gain some perspective. One activity I remember enjoying as a boy was to sit at a bus bench near our home during the busy evening Los Angeles rush hour and watch the many varieties of people driving home from work.

I would make up imaginary stories about each of their lives. What were they having for dinner? Were they loved? Did they have a dog? So many people, so many stories . . .

Unbeknownst to me, this spontaneous activity helped me realize that others have lives—everyone has a life filled, at times, with difficulty and pain. Mine wasn't the only one. In a strange way, it was quite comforting.

Tammy recently described herself going to the mall for the same reasons. She would plop herself down on a bench and watch everything—pick up snippets of conversation, observe others' behavior or demeanors—just as an additional reminder that life goes on, despite the difficulties.

Others have found being in nature an enormous help. The vastness of the ocean, the majesty of towering mountains, the expansiveness of the rolling plains help to put one's problems into perspective.

10. Seek respite. Dr. Freudenberger's research has shown that certain seemingly positive personality traits such as commitment, dedication, perfectionism, being a giver, and possessing a willingness to work hard can contribute to burnout. In order to be a strengthened ally, it's important to find ways to let go by realizing that you can't do it all. Let others do some caring in your stead.

Peter had been caring for his young wife who had recently been diagnosed with bipolar disorder. Since Elaine's medications weren't stabilized yet, he felt uncomfortable leaving her alone. To complicate matters, however, Peter's boss had asked him to take an important business trip.

Peter turned to his mother, Ruth, for help. Ruth graciously volunteered to pinch-hit in his absence. She helped Elaine make plans for daily activities during her depressed period and made sure she didn't spend a lot of time home alone worrying.

Because of Ruth's generous offer of help, not only was Peter able to achieve his goals during his trip, but he actually experienced it as a vacation from his caregiving duties.

Depending on the illness's severity, you may experience yourself as being on 24-hour watch. This is an exhausting and impossible proposition. Build a caregiving team consisting of yourself, other family members, friends, and professionals to help in dealing with your loved one's illness.

Rosalynn Carter wrote of an instance in which a national organization, the Interfaith Volunteer Caregivers, helped a postman whose depressed wife had been released from the hospital after a suicide attempt just a week before Christmas. "Will was told that he could not leave her alone," Mrs. Carter wrote. "The holidays are particularly dangerous for people suffering from severe depression." The Interfaith Volunteer Caregivers organized a team of trained volunteers to sit with Will's wife around the clock, since he was unable to take time off from work during the busiest mail season of the year.

In order to avoid burnout, you must reach out to others.

11. Be mindful of your physical health. You can't be of much help if you're depleted and exhausted yourself, so be sure to eat well and get enough sleep. The same goes for any physical ailments that may be bothering you. Pay attention to your own physical status and seek medical care for any problems you may have. Avoid drugs, alcohol, or smoking, as they further undermine your health.

Exercise is an excellent way to maintain health and reduce stress. Even if you can't get to the gym regularly, an aerobics video, a brisk walk, or a stint pulling weeds can do wonders to restore your energy.

12. Make use of the relaxation response. Biofeedback, yoga, meditation, listening to music, even washing your car can relieve stress and help you relax on a regular basis.

Central to most relaxation exercises is your awareness of your breathing. By focusing on your breath, you trigger the body-mind connection. There is no right or wrong way of doing this. Breathing is a natural—indeed, an essential—part of life that usually occurs outside your awareness.

The following is a brief "mindfulness" exercise that will help you to relax in five minutes. This technique simply asks you to pay attention to your breathing by focusing on it. You may consider making an audiotape of it to use whenever you want.

Find a comfortable position, either sitting or lying down. Take three deep breaths. Now note the point at which your breath enters your body. Is it your mouth? Your nose? Pay attention to whether your breath feels warm or cool, heavy or light, gentle or strong. Let yourself breathe in and out, being aware of the point of entry.

If you find your mind wandering, don't worry. It's the natural action of the mind to drift. The relaxation response occurs by your choice to return to focusing on the breath. So just bring yourself back to the point at which you notice the breath entering your body.

Now pay attention to any tension in your body. Mentally scan yourself, starting with your chest and the in-and-out movement of your lungs as you breathe. Then sense your neck, shoulders, head, arms, torso, back, thighs, and legs. If you are aware of any tension anywhere in your body, breathe into it. Again, if your mind wanders, simply bring it back to your body and your breath.

Using exercises such as this one, you will find that you are more relaxed, and therefore have more energy to deal with the vicissitudes of your loved one's depression. You will find additional books that contain other meditations such as this listed in Appendix 1.

13. Deal with your frustration. You may find yourself quickly frustrated by minor provocations, and later may wonder what really set you off. A short fuse can be a sign of burnout associated with taking undue responsibility (see next section). Unfortunately, however, reacting negatively to every setback will quickly leave you frustrated and can contribute to the very burnout you want to avoid.

If the suggestions I've listed here do not work for you, this is a sign that you may be needing more emotional support in the form of a support group or a private therapist. After all, depression can be a major illness, and you may need help coping with it.

14. Self-care and setting limits. As I explained earlier, it's important to recognize that you can't do it all. Often caregivers believe, "If I just do one more thing, the situation will improve." In fact, when someone you love is depressed, there is always "one more thing," and your responsibilities can seem endless. Identify when you're feeling overwhelmed—the signs of burnout listed on page 65 will help you—and be firm in your resolve as to what you can and can't do.

Grace was able to set limits in a gentle, loving way with her friend Judy, who was experiencing a bad case of the blues after her boyfriend walked out. Judy would call nightly, talking for hours about her loss. Grace was happy to be available for her best friend, but found the long hours on the phone exhausting. Finally she said to Judy, "I love talking to you, but I need to unwind after work or I don't sleep well. If I'm on the phone with you after ten P.M., I get too tired. Let's hang up by ten o'clock."

Grace's approach worked because she explained why she needed to cut off conversation at a certain hour. She described how Judy's state was impacting her, and Judy could hear that. Consequently, Judy respected Grace's request since it spoke to Grace's needs and was not a criticism of Judy.

When you learn to set limits, you will have an easier time seeking respite, caring for your own health, maintaining the patterns of your life, and letting go, thereby diminishing your chances of experiencing burnout.

REASONABLE EXPECTATIONS

When someone you love is depressed, you may feel torn about how involved you should get in his or her care. What is reasonable for you to expect of yourself as a strengthened ally? What should you expect of your loved one? When is it appropriate to step in, and when should you allow your loved one to do for himself?

What works for you now may be wrong for another family, another family member, or even for you as circumstances shift. Nevertheless, in defining your role, there are certain pitfalls that you would be wise to avoid.

TAKING TOO MUCH RESPONSIBILITY

It is easy for you to take undue responsibility or become overinvolved in your loved one's depression. You may hover, as if his every decision and movement must be monitored. You may listen for every word, to see if the depression is returning or deepening. At its most extreme, taking undue responsibility conjures images of treating your loved one as if he were still a child, unable to make a move without you.

What makes this so difficult is that your overinvolvement may arise from a deep longing and frustration for the situation to ameliorate itself faster. Your anxiety and feelings of helplessness may trigger your need for greater control.

Unfortunately, however, this behavior cheats your loved one of retaining and maintaining as much control over his life as possible. Paradoxically, when you take undue responsibility, it may reinforce your loved one's staying in exactly the position you wish he would leave—that is, stuck in his depression. If you take over, you may achieve just the opposite of what you had intended.

If you find that this is happening, it's time for both of you to work on the relationship in consultation with your family's counselor, psychologist, or psychiatrist. Taking too much responsibility can be an unproductive—even dangerous—pattern of relating, and it's best to address it directly. In Chapter 5, you'll find some other helpful suggestions for how to disengage yourself.

SELF-BLAME

Taking too much responsibility can also be linked to your blaming yourself in an unconscious, subtle way for your loved one's depression.

Toward the end of his life, my father would ruminate on the mistakes he made in dealing with my mom's depression. "If only we hadn't moved from Chicago," he would lament, or "I should never have sold the cleaning business. It kept her involved and happy." Sometimes he would add, "Remember that time you came over, and we had planned to treat her at the hospital, but in the last minute I couldn't do it? I thought to myself, 'Who and I to take another person's life from them—their choice?' I know now I was wrong."

My dad had so many regrets and second guesses in his desperate attempts to explain the unexplainable. The "I shouldn't haves" and the "If onlys" were devastating to him.

Early on, I would attempt to reassure him that he had done the best he could in a difficult situation. But later I came to realize that my dad's constant self-blame came out of a desperate need to retain some semblance of control in the face of an untenable situation. "If I had been a better husband," he seemed always to be saying, "maybe this never would have happened."

Taking too much responsibility, as my father did, may eventually boomerang and lead you to the same feelings that your depressed loved one is confronting. It is a strange irony that the closeness of you to your loved one may result in a "misery loves company" scenario. I'm sure that's not what you have in mind in becoming a strengthened ally.

We all make decisions that may appear wrong in hindsight. But at the time, they were the best that we could do.

We are limited in our abilities to control all the pain and suffering that may unfold from a particular decision, whether wrong or right. We can be responsible for our *efforts* to do the best we can in the moment, but we can't control the *outcome*—what happens as a result of these efforts and actions—though we'd like to believe otherwise.

BECOMING AN ENABLER

I was often called upon to provide excuses for my mother's glaring absences from holiday celebrations, birthday parties, weddings, and other family gatherings. Usually, I would say that she was "sick in bed" with some sort of stomach upset, headache, or cold. In effect, I was acting as an enabler.

The term "enabler" has been popularized by the alcoholism/drug recovery movement. It refers to behaving in a way that makes it possible for an individual to continue with his or her problem or allow it to go untreated. In my case it meant protecting my mother from the disapproval of others by using falsehoods, little white lies, or other subterfuges to hide or deny the truth. For instance, if I explained why my mother couldn't attend a family function by saying, "Mom didn't feel well this morning. She woke up with a cold," I was acting as an enabler to protect my mother from the stigmatizing elements of her illness.

Another aspect of enabling is that it allows us to unconsciously keep at bay the emotional strain of a loved one's illness. My conscious motivation was to protect my mother. Ironically, though, often it served to protect *me* from the pain of my own disappointment or from the truth of how difficult and hurtful the situation really was.

I now know that a better response would have been to find a way to express the truth without being hurtful and without embarrassing my mom. But I was in a double bind. I could not disclose my mother's true emotional state without my father's support. And I risked alienating my father by revealing our family secret. The problems begin to turn on themselves. Stigma fuels secrecy, which can lead to denial and enabling, all in the service of maintaining an illusion that everything is O.K.

If you find yourself in a similar situation, you might get used to rehearsing a statement such as "Jack's not feeling well, but mostly it's because of his depression." Otherwise, it's easy to find yourself going along with the cover-up as I did. Most important, you and your loved one need to talk to each other about how best to convey the true nature of the depression without being destructive to the relationship.

What if your loved one asks you to cover up the truth or to lie? "Don't you dare tell anyone what happened to me," he might say.

In this case, your response might be "I cannot lie for you. It's too devastating. We'll have to find another way to deal with this." A psychotherapist or clergyman can be helpful in sorting out a reasonable solution.

The danger in becoming an enabler is that you may fail to recognize the true nature of your loved one's depression and fall into a form of denial that can blind you to his need for psychological help.

DENIAL

There can be a fine line between not wanting your loved one to be embarrassed and the denial of a problem that warrants attention.

Dennis, the father of one of my patients, had been in denial about the true severity of his son's depression. "Brian is a little depressed," Dennis had admitted to me during a family session, early in the twenty-six-year-old's treatment. Dennis wanted to believe that Brian was O.K., even though he continued to pay his adult son's rent and provide him with a monthly allowance.

Then, one evening, Dennis attended a 12-step meeting with Brian. Afterward they had dinner at a restaurant. Feeling good about the time they had spent together, Dennis suggested that they return to Brian's apartment for some coffee. It had been several months since they had relaxed together.

"Let's not, Dad," Brian protested.

"Aw, c'mon. Just for twenty minutes," Dennis insisted. "Besides, I have to use the john."

When Dennis walked into his son's apartment, he gasped in horror. The place was in utter chaos. Filthy dishes and clothing were strewn about. Ashtrays overflowed with hundreds of stubbed-out cigarette butts. The bathroom reeked so badly that he couldn't bear to use it. Legions of cockroaches scurried across the floor when he turned on the kitchen light.

It was at that moment that Dennis had to face that his son was not just "a little depressed," and would need much more help. He had been pretending that Brian's condition did not warrant medication and that the young man could live independently. He had wanted to believe that things were O.K., but now there was no denying that they weren't.

This upsetting event helped Dennis break through his denial. He now saw that he had to take a more active role in Brian's care. What's more, he was not going to run interference for him anymore.

◆

A strengthened ally is a person who has had to learn from the roller coaster of emotions and experiences that must be addressed when someone he or she loves is depressed. Often, being a strengthened ally means having the ability to enjoy simple pleasures in the face of uncertainty. At other times, it means sharing your fears and struggles with someone you trust. It can also mean letting go the reins and having faith in your loved one's ability to cope.

Through it all, a strengthened ally does what he can to learn from his mistakes and celebrate the small gifts that life bestows. With this deepened awareness coupled with glimmers of hopefulness we can stand by the side of our depressed loved ones and endeavor to make a difference.

◆

CHAPTER 5

Comforting Your Depressed Loved One

In the last sequence of the movie *Driving Miss Daisy*, Jessica Tandy, in the title role, sits at a table in a nursing home. She is worn and withered with age. Her trusted and loyal employee, Hoke, played by Morgan Freeman, visits her, as he does every week. He is quite old himself. The patience with which he sits and deals with the ramblings of her mind conveys the feeling that these two people have shared much history. Indeed, Hoke can track the trajectory of Miss Daisy's thoughts, even when they seem to veer in seemingly unintelligible directions.

At one point during their visit, Hoke urges Miss Daisy to eat her slice of pumpkin pie. It's one of her favorites.

She doesn't respond, but simply sits there.

In this quiet moment, it feels as if the movie stops. We hold our breath, waiting to see what will unfold. And then, imperceptibly, gently, Freeman leans forward, picks up the fork, and delicately feeds Miss Daisy some pie.

At that moment the viewer recognizes that Miss Daisy's worst fears—including those that are unimaginable to her now because of her deteriorated state but are in the awareness of the audience—will never be realized. Hoke will be there for her until the very end.

When I watch that scene—and I've seen it several times—I instantly burst into tears, knowing that the moment captures both hope and dread. We all hope for someone to be there for us, unconditionally, and we all dread that somehow this will not come to pass—that we will be abandoned in our infirmity.

This fear of abandonment is endemic to the human condition, but it is also a large part of the black cloud that hovers over a depressed individual—especially if she has experienced a real abandonment. She fears being alone; she fears that everything will somehow irretrievably disappear—her health, her job, her life. She fears—no, she *believes*—that she will become unimportant, worthless, and expendable, that ultimately she will be forsaken by those whom she loves.

These fears of your loved one can be hard on you. They were certainly hard on me. I remember when my mother would describe how alone she felt. Although we loved and cared about her, we just couldn't get through the gloom that would descend around her. Sometimes while at school I would find my mind drifting to images of her at home, alone and miserable in bed. I would worry. My stomach would knot, and I would gaze out the window, deep in thought. I felt guilty, responsible. I had to leave her every day to

go to school. I had no answer to her complaints,
calls . . . nobody cares."

As a teenager, I felt helpless to console my mother. I no
that there are ways to comfort your depressed loved one ti
enhance intimacy and lead to trust. But first and foremost, you
must address the fear of abandonment in your interactions with
her. As William Styron makes clear in his memoir *Darkness Visible,*
"It may require on the part of friends, lovers, family, admirers, an
almost religious devotion to persuade the sufferers [of depression]
of life's worth, which is so often in conflict with a sense of their
own worthlessness, but such devotion has prevented countless
suicides."

WHAT NOT TO SAY

At times most of us will respond to our depressed loved one's complaints and fears with defensiveness, frustration, and denial. This is
natural, for often these complaints are frightening and upsetting, if
not wounding to us. If your depressed loved one cries, as my
mother did, "Nobody cares," your initial response might be, as
mine was, "That's not true! I care," or "Your friends care. Your parents care," and so on.

Answering in that way, however, you take the complaint literally and are addressing the specific content, not the fear of abandonment that underlies it. Unfortunately, your loved one may hear
the defensiveness behind your reassurances and may retort angrily
with statements such as "You don't understand." She may then
point out to you all the minute ways in which you have demonstrated that you don't care. An argument that shifts the focus from
your loved one's pain and fear to your perceived emotional wound
can ensue. She has slighted your caring, and this hurts you.

The result: She feels isolated in her pain and you feel criticized and unappreciated, even angry. These are the seeds of caregiver burnout.

Other well-intended but ultimately counterproductive communications include

- "Snap out of it!"
- "You'll be fine."
- "There, there. It's not that bad."
- "Sure I understand; I experienced the same problems myself."
- "Just try a little harder."
- "God never gives you more than you can bear."

These statements can feel distancing, patronizing, and judgmental. Although spoken in an attempt to reassure, a depressed individual may experience them as placating remarks that push her away and leave her feeling emotionally alone—abandoned.

There is a better way to respond, one that may require you to learn some new behaviors, including a willingness to withhold your initial impulses and consider other approaches to the situation. Your ability to comfort your depressed loved one may depend on your taking four crucial steps:

- developing the "observer's mind"
- appreciating the wisdom and the pain of an empathic silence
- learning to mirror and validate your loved one's feelings
- acting as a source of constancy—permanence—to help your loved one understand that you will not abandon her

Let's look at these steps more closely.

THE OBSERVER'S MIND

The observer's mind is the ability to detach yourself so that you respond to the feelings behind your loved one's statements rather than to their literal content. How can you do this when you're so close to each other? It's not an easy task, but it is possible.

We are so used to listening to words that sometimes we forget there are other ways of communicating and experiencing feelings. When in the observer's mind, you notice your loved one's facial expressions, hand gestures, body language, and tone of voice without regard to what she is saying. The observer's mind reflects back what it sees without judgment or evaluation, as in "It looks like Joan is angry," or "Ron seems lost and confused."

A technique that I practiced with my mom was simply to pay attention to her hands while she spoke to see if I could understand what *they* were saying. Was she wringing them? Did they seem limp? Lifeless? Were her fingers balled up in a fist? No matter what her words said, I gleaned a lot of additional information about her emotional state—whether she was anxious, withdrawn, or angry—from these simple observations.

The purpose of using the observer's mind is to avoid personalizing what your loved one is saying so that you are not drawn into an argument that neither of you wants. Using this skill will help you forestall the inevitable lament, spoken much later, "How did we get into that argument anyway?" At those times, both of you are exhausted, emotionally depleted in your attempt to salvage some closeness after a difficult, futile encounter.

When you are in the observer's mind, your goal is to recognize what your loved one is feeling without reacting personally. This position requires that you simply look and listen without responding immediately to what your loved one is saying, that you remain—for the time being, at least—in silence. It's not an easy proposition when you're feeling provoked, but it's an essential one.

Such an empathic silence is part of the second step to comforting your loved one. This is not the "silent treatment," which communicates an emotional distancing, however, but rather an attempt to connect with your loved one without engaging in the content of her communications.

THE WISDOM AND PAIN OF SILENCE

In the heat of anger, there can be little or no empathy. And without empathy, you cannot give comfort. As Daniel Goleman writes in *Emotional Intelligence,* "Empathy requires enough calm and receptivity so that the subtle signals of feeling from another person can be received and mimicked by one's own emotional brain." When you are dealing with a depressed individual, that calmness and receptivity can be achieved by empathic silence.

I first learned about the value of silence from my older brother. Before he left for graduate school at Oxford University and the long stretches of darkness descended upon our home, I remember that whenever he became annoyed with my thirteen-year-old antics, he would fall silent. He simply would not respond to any of my comments. Later, when he was in a better mood or if he just decided to relent, he would tell me that he was practicing "the wisdom of silence."

Being ten years my senior, I thought that my brother's silences were ennobling acts of power and discipline. As a typical preteen, I could no more control my impulses than I could my hormones!

After my brother left, and my mother became more consistently depressed, I learned to recall the memory of what I perceived to be his strength during difficult and accusatory conversations with her. I remember those moments well. I would turn the knob and open the door to total darkness. The air in her room would feel stale, damp—as if I had cracked open a humidor that had been sealed for a long, long time. But before I entered my mother's room in hopes of helping to lift her spirits, I knew that first I would have to endure her unpredictable moods. So, I practiced—as I listened or observed, as I cried or raged inside—"the wisdom of silence . . . the wisdom of silence . . ." in a mantralike prayer when she blamed me for all of the unhappiness in her life.

Many years later, I faced the emotional residue of chanting that phrase while watching the movie version of Chaim Potok's novel *The Chosen,* which concerns the assimilation conflicts in an Orthodox Jewish family. The phrase my brother had used, which I repeated as if it were a lifebuoy and an anchor, was taken from the Talmud, the Jewish compendium of traditions, laws, and legend. But he didn't use the complete phrase, which is "the wisdom and *the pain* of silence."

Hearing these words uttered with anguish and sorrow by the rabbi upon learning that his oldest, most gifted son was abandoning his studies shook me to my core. I wept, remembering with exquisite detail the emotionally horrifying threats of suicide, the murderous rages, the surly comments directed at me and others in our family that my mother discharged while in her depressed state.

When someone you love is depressed, you endure in silence both pain and sorrow in the hope of being for the person you love a strengthened ally, a source of support and help. Nevertheless, the pain of that silence is at the heart of the challenges you face.

Inwardly, you are deeply affected by the content of what is being said. It burns and throbs, and none of us can pretend that remaining empathically silent does not impact us emotionally. But acknowledging the pain of what you are witnessing and the ache in your heart for your loved one is an essential ingredient in what makes this an empathic—and not a hardened—silence. Moreover, you are making that acknowledgment without reacting in the moment.

Of course, this is impossible if there is an emergency that calls for action, such as a suicide attempt. But these events are much rarer than the day in, day out arguments and complaints that develop when someone you love is depressed.

Indeed, you may ask, and rightly so: If the emotional price is so high, what is the wisdom of such a silence? Who needs it? I know it seems paradoxical, but in truth, when your depressed love one is in the throes of an episode filled with rage and destructiveness, engaging in an apparently "rational" conversation about what is being said is futile and absurd. (If there is physical danger, empathic silence would not be the best response. In that case, swift, appropriate action is called for, as described on p. 112.)

Often, once the episode has passed, your loved one, like an alcoholic who has blacked out, won't remember what she said. Moreover, if you were to bring up what was said during these rages, in all likelihood it would either crush the fragile détente or bring on a new episode. Neither situation is desirable.

As I innocently came to understand, your role in these moments is to be a beacon of light, flashing the proximity of the shore without comment. The silent beam does no harm. It simply says, "I'm here; I'm listening; I care." It offers a semblance of connection, showing the way toward safety.

Later, when the mood has lifted or cycled down to a quieter level, you can follow your loved one's lead and talk about what she remembers. In these moments, the "reason" for the explosion often seems irrelevant and is best left alone.

At times, your loved one may take offense at your silence. It could trigger her rage or annoyance. If this should occur, I suggest you respond by saying, "I just want to listen. When you're through, I'll be glad to share my feelings. Right now I want to pay attention to you."

In practicing the wisdom of silence, I learned a small but important lesson: I didn't have to react automatically to what my

mother was saying when she was depressed. Fighting the
to jump in can be a small victory for you, and it has the doub.
vantage of allowing your loved one to feel heard. Perhaps this sh
ple lesson can be a source of consolation to you as well in your
attempts to comfort your loved one.

VALIDATION AND PERMANENCE

Developing the observer's mind and learning the wisdom and pain
of silence are attempts to detach yourself from feeling personally
attacked when your loved one is criticizing, vituperating, or ranting. From this emotional stance it is easier to take the next steps in
comforting your loved one: mirroring and validating her feelings.

Once you have been able to achieve some objectivity, it is much
easier to deal directly with your loved one's abandonment feelings.

The best way to convey your caring is to validate your loved
one's feelings. You do that by "mirroring," reflecting back what she
is expressing on an emotional level, not necessarily a content level.
For example, if she says to you, "I feel exhausted," a reasonable
reply might be "Honey, maybe you need to take a nap." You would
be responding to the *content* of her complaint by making a concrete
suggestion. Your loved one bristles because you've chosen to give
advice when all she wants is to be heard and understood.

But if you were to say, "Oh, honey, you sound truly weary,"
you would be validating or mirroring your loved one's emotions.
As a result, she would feel understood and would have a sense of
an emotional connection with you.

I have found that there are no words more soothing to a depressed individual than these sorts of validating statements. So
when your loved one complains that "no one cares," rather than
protesting, "But I do," you might say, "I know it feels that way to
you right now."

Then, it's helpful to follow quickly with a second statement: "But we'll get through this together." This is quite important, since it serves to reassure your loved one that you will not abandon her. Beyond that, it helps you to take on the role of constancy; like Hoke, you reassure your loved one that you'll be there for her, no matter what. In holding the perception of permanence, you also remind your loved one of the possibility that even though *you're* not going anywhere, *her* feelings are transitory. They may change, and tomorrow things could be better. In saying "We'll get through this together," you remind her of your dependability and you offer hope.

The following are several other familiar phrases that my depressed patients or their loved ones have related to me. These can be both a source of frustration and a wellspring of connection, depending on how you deal with them. How you respond can serve as a soothing balm to the intense emotional pain connected with depression. Your position should be to validate your loved one's feelings and to reassure her that you will not abandon her. When you do so, you will have achieved another small victory.

Remember that the depressed person's complaints are expressions of emotional pain. Don't get embroiled in a battle over the content of the statement. Stick with the feelings.

◆

- "I'm all alone."
  Don't Say: "No you're not! I'm sitting here with you right now. Doesn't my caring about you mean anything?"
  Do Say: "I know that you're feeling alone right now. Is there anything I can do to help? I'm glad to just be with you. Together we'll get through this lonely feeling."
- "Why bother? Life isn't worth living. There's no point in going on."

Don't Say: "How can you think that? You hav[e] [beau]tiful children and a great job. I love you. You [have every]thing to live for."

Do Say: "I know it feels that way to you right now, but I want you to know that you matter to me and you matter to the children. We'll get through this hopeless feeling together."

• "I'm dragging everyone else down with me."

Don't Say: "No you're not. You see? I'm fine. I had a good day today. And besides, I'm doing everything in the world to help you."

Do Say: "I know it feels that way to you right now. And yes, at times it is difficult for both of us, but we'll get through this burdened feeling together."

• "What would it be like if I wasn't here anymore?"

Don't Say: "Don't talk crazy! What's wrong with you?"

Do Say: "I would miss you terribly. You're important to me. I want to grow old with you. We'll get through this together."

• "I'm expendable."

Don't Say: "If you felt better about yourself, you wouldn't say stupid things like that."

Do Say: "I know you're feeling worthless right now, but we'll get through this."

• "Nothing I do is any good. I'll never amount to anything."

Don't Say: "What are you saying? You're a highly respected engineer! You're a great dad! You're blowing everything out of proportion."

Do Say: "I know it's upsetting when things don't work out the way you want them to. It's upsetting for me too. Failure feelings are really painful. We'll get through this together."

- "How long an I going to feel this way? It feels as if I'll never get better."

  Don't Say: "C'mon, nothing lasts forever. You know better than that."

  Do Say: "I know it's scary to be in so much pain. Feelings come and go. We'll get through this together."

- "My shrink wants me to see a psychiatrist for medication. I feel like I'll be cheating if I go on antidepressants—like I'm admitting I'm not strong enough to beat this."

  Don't Say: "I want to support your efforts to get better, and I don't want to tell you what to do."

  Do Say: "We know that the best hope for successful treatment is a combination of medication and therapy. I know this is a job, but we'll get through it together."

- "I don't want to take medication. It means I'm really sick."

  Don't Say: "If the doctor thinks you're that ill, maybe you should do it . . ."

  Do Say: "I don't want you to suffer from depression any longer than you have to since we know part of this is biological."

- "Yeah, I was able to get up and go to work today, but I don't think I did anything worthwhile because I was anxious and distracted."

  Don't Say: "Why are you focusing on the negative?"

  Do Say: "I know it seems like not much was accomplished but sometimes that's the depression talking. Honey, you may not be the most reliable reporter of your successes."

- "I get in the elevator and smile at my coworkers, but they don't acknowledge my presence. It's like I don't even exist."

Don't Say: "Don't be ridiculous! Why does the world have to revolve around you?"

Do Say: "That must make it so hard for you to show up at work, though it's hard to imagine that everyone in the elevator is focused on you."

- "I can't talk to my parents about what's really going on with me. I don't want them to know or worry."

Don't Say: "I'm glad you can talk to me."

Do Say: "We need all the help we can get. I'm glad to go with you when you talk to them. I don't want you to suffer alone."

◆

I've only listed a few scenarios here, but I've heard these or some variation of them repeated many, many times among caregivers and their depressed loved ones.

Your loved one may verbalize her pain in a way that touches a hot button in you and ultimately escalates into a disconnection between the two of you. In order to avoid that eventuality, you might want to write what your loved one often says when she's feeling down, and your typical response.

- Your loved one says: _____

_____

_____

- Your typical response: _____

_____

_____

Now, referring to the earlier examples, try reframing your response so that it both validates your loved one's emotions and reassures her of your continuing presence.

- Your new response: _____
_____
_____

SETTING REASONABLE LIMITS

Reasonable limits help create a feeling of safety. They let your loved one know what you will do if her behavior becomes unacceptable or life-threatening. Limit setting is comforting because often, when a person is severely depressed, everything feels out of control. Following through on limits that you have previously agreed upon together helps your loved one know that she does not have to literally hit bottom to get help. This results in her feeling more secure and in her understanding that you are in this together.

It is a common practice for therapists to make limit-setting contracts with their severely depressed clients. The patient agrees to call her therapist when she is feeling suicidal or when other behaviors that they have identified in advance as dangerous markers begin to be played out. For instance, Marsha knew to call me whenever she found herself skipping meals. We had already established that this could trigger a depressive episode.

In order to set limits, it's important to define destructive behavior. Let your loved one know in advance what you'll tolerate and what you won't. (In Chapter 4, Grace lovingly set a limit regarding telephone time with her friend Judy.) Also, be clear about the consequences and consistent in following through. Your family's therapist or psychiatrist can help you work out guidelines that you'll all feel comfortable with.

Practice setting up in advance with each other the limits of an argument. My clients Jean and Glen established such a routine and it helped to keep their conflicts from escalating. Glen had had an extramarital affair some twenty years earlier. Jean had never let go of her wound or forgiven him for his transgression.

Ever since Jean had become depressed, she had been ultrasensitive to any action on Glen's part that was even faintly reminiscent of his prior infidelity. If he talked to a female acquaintance at a party, Jean, in her morose state, would interpret that as his becoming too friendly with her. Her first impulse was to bring up the past, triggering a depressive episode and causing a terrible row.

In therapy, I advised Glen that certain words or topics would trigger Jean's reaction and his own hurt feelings that she had never forgiven him for the affair. The couple agreed that if this came up between them again, Glen would take a walk around the block. This time-out served to defuse the conflict and preserve the peace in their household.

Jean and Glen also used a technique called reframing to set limits. Reframing entails placing a painful, wounding occurrence in a new perspective—seeing it in a new light. When Jean was able to situate Glen's infidelity in the context of the thousands of ways he had stood by her in the twenty years since the incident, she was able to say to herself, "On the whole, we've had a wonderful marriage with just this one transgression." This helped reduce the frequency and severity of her depressive episodes.

Finally, setting limits can apply to yourself as well as to your loved one. As Daniel Goleman explains in *Emotional Intelligence,* feelings are contagious: "We transmit and catch moods from each other in what amounts to a subterranean economy of the psyche." We do this by unconsciously and imperceptibly mimicking the subtle gestures, tone of voice, and facial expressions—the nonverbal communicators—that others display.

In the face of sharing your loved one's pain and expressing

empathy for her plight, the ability to maintain your own boundaries can help you deal with an individual who overwhelms you with insatiable feelings of emptiness.

Because of work and family pressures, Eric promised himself that he would only stop in to see his depressed father fifteen minutes each morning before going to the office, and fifteen minutes after dinner each evening. That seemed manageable to him, and he felt less resentful in making those brief visits. Maintaining reasonable boundaries is part of becoming a strengthened ally. Besides, if you feel burned out and trapped within your own depression, it is difficult for you to offer comfort to your loved one. Limit setting is a basic way that you can convey stability, safety, and a sense of permanence.

USING FAMILY MEETINGS
TO RESOLVE CONFLICTS

A family meeting is a problem-solving tool to improve communication. This is an occasion when you set aside a specific time to discuss a topic of concern, either solely between you and your loved one or among close, concerned family members. These meetings can be held regularly—once a week or once a month—or by appointment when unexpected emergencies make them necessary. Be sure to set the agenda before beginning. If you try to cover too much ground in one meeting, the issues may become muddled.

Avoid confusing the discussion by bringing in extraneous complaints and ancient history. This may be difficult if you have pent-up feelings, but it is necessary if the meeting is to be successful. See to it that phone calls or other distractions don't interrupt your session and stick to a limited time-frame—forty-five minutes or so.

During these meetings, each person must get equal time to

have his or her say. Each must feel heard. Equality helps your loved one feel important and engenders a sense of responsibility.

Be careful how you explain your state of mind. Inappropriately expressed feelings, including accusations and disdain, can cause big arguments. When you let your loved one know that you understand her position, she will be more likely to cooperate in the meeting.

Don't hide your true feelings. Avoid saying, "I hate to bother you because you're so down," when you really mean "I can't go on like this." It's best to ask if you've made yourself clear. You can even request confirmation by asking, "What did you hear me say?"

In opening communications, proceed cautiously. If you communicate appropriately, you can build intimacy among family members. The following suggestions may be useful in setting the groundwork for a meaningful and successful conversation:

1. *Make yourselves comfortable.* It helps if you are on the same physical and emotional level. You'll feel you're on an equal footing and will believe you'll really listen to one another if you take the time to sit down and discuss your issues in a focused way.

2. *Really listen.* Listening is an active form of communication. A person who is listened to feels cared about and valued. Listening implies mutual respect. You will all need to feel listened to in order for your dialogue to be successful. If your depressed loved one cuts off you or another family member in midthought, remind her that you heard her out when it was her turn to speak; now it's only reasonable that she listen. The same, of course, applies to you and everyone else.

If after listening you feel you've been misinterpreted, you might say, "You're not hearing me." Try again. Speak calmly and explain yourself in a different way.

3. Make eye contact. Poets have called the eyes the windows to the soul. Emotions, especially love, are expressed through the eyes. From earliest infancy onward, we all understand these nonverbal cues. When you look into your loved one's eyes as you speak, you're letting her know that your attention is focused on her and her alone.

If your loved one tends to cast her eyes downward, you can gently remind her that you find it hard to know what she's feeling if she's staring at the floor. You can say, "I'm afraid I may miss what you're trying to tell me."

If she still can't look you in the eye, tell her, "It's O.K. I'll listen to you anyway." Perhaps as you continue your discussion, she'll come around. Never force her to do what she doesn't want to do.

By the same token, if you tend to avert your eyes, remind yourself of the importance of making eye contact as you speak and as you listen.

4. Ask questions in a nonthreatening way. Work with each other asking open-ended questions that contain an element of curiosity. You can say, "Help me understand what's going on with you, Janet." Keep your voice as calm as possible. This opens the way for discussion.

It's vital that all of you understand how you're feeling. If you don't, keep asking in different ways until you do-but don't badger. If you achieve only partial understanding, explain which areas are clear to you and which aren't.

If you feel angry, wait until the intensity has diminished before speaking.

5. Use mirroring. As I explained above, mirroring validates your loved one's emotional experience by communicating *your* understanding of what *she's* feeling. By mirroring your loved one's emotions, you show her that you understand and respect her.

6. *Separate character from actions.* In order to help each other feel good about the relationship and maintain self-esteem, it's important to distinguish between upsetting or frustrating behavior and general character.

Jean's work was to separate the action—Glen's unacceptable behavior, having the affair—from her thoughts that he was a despicable person for having cheated on her. She did so by reminding herself of his character: the enduring quality of his commitment to her, of his underlying goodness and love.

Stick with *your* emotions. Rather than attacking your loved one's character, it's more acceptable to say, "I feel hurt, angry, frustrated." This keeps your loved one from becoming defensive.

When you separate character from actions, you communicate that you continue to value each other, even though you may find a particular behavior difficult to accept.

7. *Clarify assumptions.* When you are feeling hurt, you can distort your loved one's words or actions. If your wife's need to take to her bed makes you furious, you might blurt out in rage, "You just can't wait to get away from me, can you?" In actuality her need may have little to do with escaping you. Indeed, just the opposite may be true: She may be trying to calm herself with quiet time in order to reconnect with you later.

Aaron Beck, the founder of cognitive-behavioral therapy, calls such underlying and possibly harmful assumptions "automatic thoughts." These thoughts create the greatest disruption in relationships because they cause us to ruminate upon and view current situations through the potentially distorting lens of past injuries.

An effective method of addressing these unspoken assumptions is by asking your loved one questions that could bring clarification. In the above situation, the upset husband might ask, "Are you saying that you want to get away from me?"

In all likelihood, his wife's response will be "Of course not. I'm

el overwhelmed. I'm trying to regroup. I don't
ve me. It helps to know you're in the next room."

ur antennae tuned to unspoken communica-
tion. Facial expressions, body language, and even silence all communicate feelings that need to be understood and articulated. Your
loved one may say, "Oh, don't worry about me. I'm just fine," but
his slumped shoulders and shuffling gait may give away his true
emotions.

9. *Express love.* Love is ongoing; anger is temporary. Despite the angry feelings that may be aired during your discussion,
it's best to find some way to express your underlying feelings of
love and caring for each other. This will cement your relationship
despite the difficulties you share. You might say, "After all, we are
still the same people we were before the depression struck. You're
still my mom, no matter what."

OTHER WAYS TO MAINTAIN INTIMACY

Until now, I have been describing how to comfort your loved one
by maintaining verbal intimacy. But there are so many other ways
of communicating your caring. Indeed, as has been drummed into
my head in every psychology course I have taken, only 7 percent of
our communication is actually dependent on our words. The remaining 93 percent is based on nonverbal cues such as facial expression, intonation, and body language.

So many of my depressed patients feel grateful just being
hugged—without words. The healing power of touch, especially
when it's mutual, is tremendous. Embracing, holding hands, gen-

tle stroking, kissing, making love—these are all ways of spreading comfort in a simple and direct way.

But getting to a point in the relationship where you're both receptive to that experience can be profoundly difficult. One way to break barriers is simply to sit together and listen to music. My parents used to watch the *Lawrence Welk Show* together. Humming the tunes in unison, they would be transported for a brief hour back to happier times. Even in my mother's bleakest days, my parents would not miss that show.

Music has a soothing power that allows both of you to be passive and to receive. In *Prozac Nation*, Elizabeth Wurtzel describes how the ragged, throaty voices of Bob Dylan and Bruce Springsteen got her through many tormented nights. Even former Senator and presidential candidate Bob Dole used Frank Sinatra's rendition of "You'll Never Walk Alone" to help him recover emotionally from the physical wounds he suffered in World War II. "When I was in rehabilitation right after the war, I played that thing thirty or forty times a day," *The New York Times* reported him explaining to his supporters during the 1996 presidential primary campaign. "I listened to it over and over and over again when I needed some help or needed some inspiration."

Another easy way to provide comfort is to follow the advice of a popular bumper sticker and "Practice random acts of kindness." Perform some small, unexpected, but thoughtful acts that will encourage a bit of cheer. Bring home some freshly baked cookies, a bouquet of flowers, a new CD. My dad used to surprise my mother with an occasional box of chocolates from See's, a local confectioner. These always reminded her of the Fanny Mae confections of her youth in Chicago. "Those were better," she would say, a smile piercing her gloom, "but these will do."

These considerate acts communicate caring and warmth without requiring elaboration or explanation. They simply stand by themselves. They also work very well if your loved one has the blues.

It's important for you and your loved one to capture those random acts of kindness that break through the depression and create a connection and intimacy. Cherish those moments of goodness and savor them. They will be of comfort to both of you and are an important part of your role as a strengthened ally.

If your loved one rejects your efforts—if she ignores them or is even hostile toward them—it's important for you to comfort yourself with the thought that at least you're doing all you can. It's hard to continue to be kind to someone when in the midst of turmoil, confusion, conflict, and misunderstanding. It may be best to remind yourself not to personalize the rejection, to ascribe it to the depression, to practice reframing, and to just let it go.

Do be aware that if the depression is related to a traumatic event such as a sexual assault or other physical attack, these simple techniques may be less effective. For deeper injuries such as these, help from a family therapist, psychologist, or psychiatrist is the best course of action.

The next several chapters discuss the most prevalent treatments for depression.

◆

CHAPTER 6

Finding Hope in Psychotherapy

MY PATIENT MIKE HAD RECENTLY RETURNED TO therapy after a series of losses: His mother had died; his company had downsized, leaving him working harder with less support; and some of his closest colleagues—genuine friends—had been let go. He was the one who had had to make many of the decisions about who would be terminated.

All of these events had depressed Mike. He joked about "survivor's guilt," he began smoking again, and he found himself increasingly relying on marijuana to get him through the night. At home he became reclusive, spending evenings and weekends puttering around in the garage. He could see that all of this was greatly affecting his relationship with Julie, his wife of twelve years. They had stopped making love or even talking. He knew he was in trouble.

We discussed the need for immediate medical intervention and came to the conclusion that along with psychotherapy, a consultation with a psychiatrist specializing in medications (a psychopharmacologist) was needed. After the consultation, a course of medication and therapy was prescribed.

Within ten days Mike was better. He literally returned to his old self before our very eyes. Mike, Julie, and I were delighted. And I joked that Mike's "miraculous" recovery reminded me of images of those old revival meetings in which the crippled threw down their crutches, exclaiming, "I can walk!" and the congregation shouted, "Hallelujah!" in response.

The good news is that 70 percent of those suffering from depression can find relief just as quickly as Mike did. There is every reason to hope that your loved one's illness will fall into this category. Even in the more difficult cases—the other 10 percent—medical and psychotherapeutic treatments can be just as successful over a longer term.

This is important for you to know because when someone you love is depressed, you may be feeling overwhelmed with anxiety and may be asking yourself questions regarding the possibility of a cure, such as the following:

- Does he need treatment?
- If so, what kind is best at first?
- Does he need more than one kind of treatment—psychotherapy and medications? Should he get these at the same time, or successively?

- How can I get him to therapy?
- How often should he go to therapy? Does that change over time—will he need to go more or less often as he pulls out of the tailspin he's in?
- Does he need medication? Will it work? Will he become dependent on it?
- What will be the side effects? Will they be just that—side effects—and not permanent problems?
- Does he need to be hospitalized?
- How long will it take before he gets better?
- How can we prevent a relapse?
- What can I expect?
- How can I help?

In this and the following chapters, I will help you sort through the many treatment options available to your loved one so that, as a strengthened ally, you can support him in seeking and maintaining a treatment plan that works for him.

Remember, despite beliefs to the contrary, modern treatments for depression are highly effective. When adhered to, they save friendships, marriages, and lives.

WORKING ON THE BLUES

If your loved one just has a case of the blues, he may not need psychotherapy or medication. There are ways that he can help himself feel better and that you can encourage him to get over his slump. As discussed in Chapter 2, the blues are not the same as a full depression. When your loved one is coping with the blues, he is still able to incorporate suggestions and take actions that actually help him feel better.

As we saw in the previous chapter, encouraging and supportive statements that you make can relieve your loved one's anxieties. Moreover, you can invite him to pay attention to his negative thoughts. Once he becomes aware of how self-critical he sounds, he may be able to recognize how he has altered reality.

For instance, if after losing a big account he declared, "I'm a failure. I was never any good at sales, and I'll never be any good!" you can gently remind him that

- You understand why he's feeling so down. It's awful to lose a big account, and it's natural to feel upset about it.
- He has lost accounts before but had figured out creative solutions that turned out better than he expected.
- There were times when he was quite successful. You might ask him to recount some of his earlier triumphs.
- Most likely, he will be successful again once he gets over this loss.

This dose of support and reality may remind your loved one of the transitory nature of most events in our lives, and thus help him regain his equilibrium. On the other hand, the blues can turn into a full-blown depression if one ruminates on negative thoughts, thereby triggering a downward spiral. Consequently, it may help if you reframe these perceptions, and also suggest sharing an enjoyable activity together. Social interactions are great diversions, as are comedies or action-adventure movies. So are exercise and sports. See Chapter 10 for further ideas on activities to dispel the blues.

ENCOURAGING YOUR LOVED ONE TO SEEK TREATMENT

If your efforts seem not to penetrate your loved one's gloom, then it's important to help him seek treatment. Depression is a *family illness*.

The depression itself—the lethargy, the pessimism, the sense of hopelessness—can make it difficult for your loved one to motivate himself to reach out. It may, therefore, fall to you to encourage him to get the help he may desperately need.

This may be harder than it seems. As my father explained it, he just found it too difficult to take away the freedom of the person he loved by hospitalizing her. My father is not alone. According to the National Institute of Mental Health, only a third of those needing treatment for depression actually receive it.

You, your loved one, other family members and the health-care team all play important roles in his recovery. As University of Florida biopsychiatrist Mark S. Gold explains in his book, *The Good News About Depression*, "The days of dealing directly with a patient, administering medication and/or therapy along with an occasional therapy session with the family, are gone." Today, the standard of care requires that the therapist treating a depressed patient also treat the entire social fabric of his life. Your involvement is essential. Indeed, you and other family members may even participate in the therapy. Dr. Gold writes, "The patient, the doctor, and the family are all part of the treatment plan, and that plan can't work if everyone involved doesn't understand what the treatment is and what to expect."

You have to believe that helping your loved one get treatment can be one of the most important steps you take. What can you do? In part, that depends on your relationship with the individual and the severity of the depression.

YOUR CHILD

Eight-year-old Teddy was exhibiting signs of childhood depression after his parents' angry separation and his father's abrupt withdrawal from the family several months earlier. As the self-proclaimed new "man in the family," he began acting out as if he were an irate parent, bossing around his little brother, yelling at him and hitting him. He seemed to regress emotionally. Little things, like his brother's spilling some milk, would send him into paroxysms of tears. He would chew on the corner of his shirt collar in an attempt to calm himself.

When his mother, Emily, tried to comfort him, he would push her away. But at other times he became clingy and whiny. "The only time he lets me get close to him is when he's ill," Emily complained. Often, it's hard to comprehend that your child is depressed.

The challenge in helping your child receive treatment is recognizing and accepting that he is depressed in the first place. As I explained in Chapter 2, the symptoms of depression in a child may be masked by normal developmental behavior such as clinginess or rebelliousness. Also, bear in mind that attention deficit disorders and other learning disabilities have a depressive component because of the frustrations they create for many school-age children. Once the disorder is properly diagnosed and treated, the anxiety and depression linked to the frustration is significantly lessened.

A depressed child may manifest the usual signs of depression such as sadness and sleep disturbances or he may convey his symptoms as physical complaints that have no apparent medical basis or, like Teddy, in aggressive, destructive behavior. A teacher, counselor, or clergyman may remark that your youngster doesn't seem himself—he shows no enthusiasm for his classwork, and he no longer takes joy in the play, activities, or hobbies that once gave him great pleasure.

If you suspect that your child is depressed, your first step is to obtain a thorough physical exam from your family's pediatrician. In Chapter 1, I discussed some of the many illnesses that may manifest as depression. If there are no physical indications, the physician can refer your youngster and/or your family to an appropriate therapist for treatment.

YOUR TEENAGER

Teenagers may be reluctant to get help, especially if their parents are pushing them toward it. They may feel embarrassed to be seen as different or they may believe their newfound autonomy is being impinged upon by a parent's insistence on delving into their emotional state. "You just don't understand" is a common cry.

The first step in helping your adolescent is to assess whether the conflicts the two of you may be having go beyond normal teen rebellion. You may begin to see signs of decreased interest in sports or activities, poor school performance, hanging out with a new group of friends, disjointed sleep patterns, and/or signs of alcohol or drug use. I have learned to suggest to parents that they trust their intuition when assessing whether their adolescent is depressed. It's better to err on the side of caution than to regret not responding soon enough.

If your teen complains, "You just don't understand," your reply could be "Honey, maybe you're right. Let's get some help!" Ninety-five percent of the adolescents I've worked with experience relief at the suggestion of getting help. They are in pain.

If your child is more resistant to your efforts, enlist the aid of the school counselor and your youngster's friends and peers. You may need to consult a mental health professional for advice on how to most effectively deal with the situation. Some approaches used with depressed adults also work with teens. You may want to try some of the suggestions in the following sections.

If no other method works, some experts recommend "getting tough" with depressed teens: seeing to it that they receive outpatient treatment or that they're hospitalized or placed in drug or residential treatment programs despite their ambivalence. This is especially likely if the youngster has attempted suicide or is abusing drugs and/or alcohol. Unless a crisis warrants otherwise it's important to try the suggestions below before embarking on such an extreme course of action.

Again, before any treatment is undertaken, a thorough physical is required.

YOUR ADULT CHILD

If your child is a young adult (roughly between the ages of eighteen and thirty) and is depressed, you may have difficulty influencing him to seek treatment. In this case, you may find it helpful to enlist his siblings, friends, or others he respects such as mentors or other family members to intercede. His relationships with these individuals may be unclouded by the normal parent-child tensions, and these people may have more success in getting through to him than you do.

One of the difficulties parents of depressed young adults face is an understandable reluctance on the child's part to give up the reins of control. There is a difference, however, between *caring about* your child and *taking care* of him. As I explained in the previous chapter, if you become overly involved, you may rob your child of the opportunity to take responsibility for his own welfare, and this can exacerbate the depression.

The first step is to communicate your concern. While respecting his independence, ask if there are ways you can help. For instance, you can say, "John, I've noticed that you seem to be ill and missing work a lot. I'm concerned that there's something more going on. I know that you pride yourself in being able to figure things out on your own. How can I act as a resource for you?"

If your child is unwilling to dialogue with you and the problems and symptoms persist, you must intercede with the help of friends, his partner, other siblings, coworkers—anyone with whom your child has a meaningful and trusting relationship. The focus of your efforts should be on how to help—not control—your child. The suggestions on p. 112 may be helpful in this situation.

If your child is over the age of thirty, most likely your relationship is no longer that of a parent, but rather more that of an intimate friend. Your loving comfort and concern coupled with respect for his autonomy can be the hallmarks of your approach to dealing with his illness.

The truth is, you may not have much influence over your child's behavior, but you certainly have influence over your own. If you are struggling with how best to deal with a depressed young adult, it may be helpful for you to consult with a therapist.

YOUR SPOUSE

It is a sign of loving and caring to note that your spouse seems depressed and might benefit from treatment. In the best of all possible worlds, he will accept your feedback and be cooperative. It may be difficult, however, for him to hear your concern. After all, you live together, and he may view such a statement as an insult, a threat, and fuel for further arguments.

My parents struggled with this issue. My father would wonder how you can have children together, raise them, work to build a future, and then decide that your life's partner is in trouble and can no longer make reasonable decisions in her best interest? Certainly, my mother did not take it well when he suggested that she get treatment. And he often lamented that he had neither the will nor the know-how to be effective in his insistence that she receive care. That obstacle was too great for him, but it does not have to be overwhelming for you.

I have often replayed in my mind—wishing it were possible to recapture what is gone forever—how my father might have been successful in overcoming my mother's reluctance. Had he been able to follow the steps I've learned and applied with my patients and their families, perhaps she would have received much-needed treatment.

The following are the steps you should consider if your spouse refuses treatment yet needs it desperately. These measures are to be tried when there is a full depression—not just the blues.

1. Be very clear in your mind that your taking charge and withstanding your loved one's protests against your interventions are an integral part of loving and caring.

2. Enlist the support of your family physician, clergyman, therapist, and/or other health-care professional to work with you.

3. Once you've gained enough internal conviction and external support, with your "team" develop a realistic plan that you will follow—no matter what.

4. Call a meeting that includes your loved one, the team, and any other close friends or family members whose support you need and can count on.

5. During the meeting iron out and agree upon the plan. Ideally, your loved one will work with you.

6. If your loved one holds to his refusal to cooperate, state what you will do. For example, "I'm prepared to take you to the hospital for an evaluation or to the doctor for treatment." At the same time, be ready to act immediately. Of course, you should also explain that you would much prefer having your loved one's cooperation to "give it a try" rather than forcing this upon him.

7. In either case, make the point that you care enough and love him enough to take whatever action is necessary to help him.

In my experience, when all of these elements—especially the emotional resolve to act—are in place, there is a good chance that your loved one will respond appropriately. He may even feel relief at your directness and strength and act like the young child who stops challenging when he realizes that you mean what you say.

Betty and Jack had just such an experience. Jack had been forced into an early retirement when his company went through a reorganization. He might have weathered that storm well—he had been looking forward to leaving his job as a regional marketing director—if not for the back surgery he suddenly required only a month after he received his not-so-golden handshake. While he convalesced from his operation, he had plenty of time to ruminate on the new, unhappy direction his life had taken. Soon he became quite depressed.

Betty watched as her husband's mood deteriorated. When he stopped shaving and getting dressed in the morning, when he began spending hours in bed, staring at the TV, she started to fear for the worst. She pleaded with Jack to get professional help, but he refused. "No, I'm fine," he would say thickly, even though his demeanor and behavior contradicted this.

Betty couldn't stand by and do nothing. But in order to have the emotional resolve to act, she needed the support of their adult children and closest friends. She talked to each of them, explaining the situation. And then she said, "I had hoped it wouldn't come to this, but I need to know if you'll be there for us, day or night. Can I call on you to be present at a family meeting or to help me take Jack to the hospital for a psychiatric evaluation?"

Everyone agreed to help out—and some even expressed gratitude for being asked. With that support, Betty had the resolve to act. She explained to Jack the problem as she saw it. "Look, honey," she said. "I'm really worried about you. I've never seen you like this. You seem very depressed. I think we need to call Dr. Marcy and get you to the hospital where they can evaluate what's going on with you."

Betty believed that she could talk to her husband calmly about his state because she had the support of her family and friends. And to her surprise, Jack simply replied, "Whatever you say."

"Do you want to call Dr. Marcy, or should we do it together?" Betty asked.

"I want you in the room with me."

As this couple readied themselves to go to the hospital, Betty explained to Jack that they would need support during this difficult time. "I'm going to tell the kids and the Campbells to meet us at the hospital so we won't be alone," she said, lifting the phone receiver. Jack and Betty were greeted at the hospital by those who loved and cared about them most.

The existence of a supportive team can be all-important; the National Institute of Mental Health makes clear in their public information bulletins, "Close relatives or friends who understand that depression is an illness and not a weakness can often convince the depressed spouse to seek treatment. . . . Sometimes, if enough people say often enough, 'We care about you, but you need professional care to feel better,' the message gets through." Here, too, it may be helpful for you to seek support for yourself from a therapist.

YOUR FRIEND

If it is a good friend who is depressed, you might find, as in the case of young adults, that you don't have as much influence as you would like. The suggestions I've made to enlist the aid of family members, coworkers, and other friends when dealing with young adults might be helpful in this situation too. Naturally, if your friend is confiding to you suicidal thoughts, you must make an effort to contact appropriate family members or take action.

AN OLDER PERSON

So often the losses inherent in aging—the death of friends and loved ones, the debilitation that comes with disease, the restrictions on a formerly robust life—can bring on a depression. It is painful but unavoidable that as your parents age, you may be called upon to parent them—to take charge of their evaluation and treatment.

Because so many physical conditions and side effects of medications can mimic and even trigger depression, it is essential that your depressed older loved one receive a thorough physical exam if symptoms of depression appear. If your loved one seems forgetful or confused, you or another trusted individual should accompany him to the doctor's office to be sure the medical history is complete and to describe all of the medications (including those purchased over the counter) he is taking.

If no physical cause is found, the physician should refer your loved one to a gerontological mental health specialist. Should your loved one require antidepressant medication, the prescribing psychiatrist or physician must be fully informed of all of the other medications being taken.

If your loved one resists treatment, you may find it helpful to follow the scenario I suggested above for a reluctant spouse. It may also be helpful for a geriatric social worker to be part of your team. My mother suffered another bout of depression after a stroke some years ago. The social worker we hired to help us deal with her situation discovered that her depression was exacerbated by the hospital's mischarting her need for thyroid medication. His participation made a great deal of difference.

WHAT TO LOOK FOR IN TREATMENT

Treatments are only as effective as your loved one's participation in them. Therefore, any therapy recommended should be one that your loved one can follow. As with any treatment, the professional your loved one consults should lay out the therapeutic goals and priorities as soon as a diagnosis is reached. These should include

- an abatement of the symptoms
- a return to "normal" function at home and at work
- the prevention of relapse

In addition, your loved one should be informed about the duration and consequences of treatment. As Mark S. Gold explains, "In psychiatry, the best patient is an educated one." In Chapter 11, I will explain in detail what you and your loved one should expect from a therapist.

EFFECTIVE PSYCHOTHERAPY

No one book can describe in any meaningful way all of the psychological therapies that can be used to help a depressed individual. There is one modality, however, cognitive-behavioral therapy, that is consistently cited in the literature as an effective tool in treating depression.

The therapist your loved one chooses doesn't need to specialize in this kind of therapy in order to be helpful. The cognitive-behavioral approach can be incorporated into many different types of clinical practice.

There is some research indicating that when someone is clinically depressed, he needs to feel that the therapist is actively involved in helping him without being overbearing. A deeply depressed individual might misinterpret a more passive therapeutic stance as a lack of caring, and that can exacerbate his condition. On the other hand, if the therapist is seemingly overinvolved in your loved one's actions, this may interfere with his taking responsibility for his own recovery. It's a fine line. All of these issues should be discussed as part of the treatment plan that you and your loved one understand and agree to.

THE COGNITIVE-BEHAVIORAL APPROACH

Cognitive-behavioral therapy was developed by a University of Pennsylvania psychiatrist, Aaron T. Beck, as an approach to dealing specifically with depression.

It is based on the theory that thoughts impact feelings and feelings impact thoughts. The therapist using this approach will help your loved one focus on self-defeating automatic thoughts such as "I'm stupid. I'm so stupid. *Stupid. Stupid. Stupid,*" and the assumptions that underlie them—those conscious beliefs that, according to Dr. Beck, "intervene between external events and an individual's emotional reaction to these events." Often, these thoughts and beliefs occur so frequently and so rapidly that we are unaware of them.

By asking questions such as "Are you stupid in every situation or is there one situation in which you didn't act stupidly in the last day, week, or month?" the therapist challenges these automatic subliminal self-critical statements. When they can be recognized and dispelled, your loved one's feelings about himself will improve.

Let's look at the case of David, a salesman who became blue after losing a valuable account. Imagine that rather than pulling out of his funk, David actually became depressed as a result of his perceived incompetence. The cognitive therapist might use David's self-defeating statement "I'm a failure. I was never any good at sales, and I'll never be any good at anything I do!" as a jumping-off point for therapy.

The therapist might approach David's negative thoughts as a scientist would analyze the hypothesis of an experiment, dividing it into its component parts and testing each part out. "You're no good as a salesman. . . . Let's see if this is true. Have you ever made any big sales?" the therapist might ask. As David recounts his successes, he discovers for himself that his thoughts may be distorted, illogical, or faulty.

Eventually, the therapist will also point out contradictions or other problems inherent in the automatic assumptions. In this case, David's underlying assumption might be that his value as a human being rests on his success in business. Again, the therapist will put this assumption to the test with questions such as "Can you tell me about some of your attributes that have nothing to do with work?" As he discusses his relationship with his daughters, David comes to see that he has value as a person, not just as a breadwinner.

As with David, when your loved one begins therapy in this mode, he and the therapist will list and then prioritize the problems they're going to deal with. The therapist will help dispel some of his initial feelings of hopelessness by working on a small problem that can be resolved quickly and easily.

"Homework" is often an integral part of the cognitive-behavioral approach. In fact, the therapist may explain to you and your loved one that it is even more important than the time spent in the therapy session. It helps both of you remain active in the therapy and encourages you both to apply what your loved one has learned in the therapy session to his outside life. It also enhances feelings of self-reliance. Those who consistently do the homework seem to recover from their depression faster.

Homework can consist of keeping a list of situations and automatic thoughts throughout the day, identifying and rating pleasurable experiences (to prove that life *is* worth living), reading material that pertains to the problems, writing, reviewing the therapy session on tape, rehearsal and role playing, and so on. Sometimes there will be assignments that you can do together. Sometimes, if your loved one agrees, it can be your task to help him by pointing out his automatic, self-critical statements.

Angie and Roger's homework assignment was to keep track of and count their negative thoughts during the week. Each evening they talked about their "findings."

"I was in the market," Angie said, "and I caught myself thinking, 'Why do I always get in the longest line?' "

"Yeah," replied Roger. "I found myself cursing myself for not being able to find a parking spot at the office."

They both laughed at the universality of their complaints and began to talk about how they could correct their thinking.

For example, Roger noted to his wife, "If you felt bad waiting at the checkout stand, imagine how the guy behind you must have felt."

As your loved one's thoughts begin to change, so will his behavior. He may practice becoming more assertive and may therefore have new, more positive thoughts about his effectiveness. David, the salesman, decided to leave a taped message for himself each evening to remind himself of the day's accomplishments on the following morning. In that way he could connect to his positive achievements if he experienced any setbacks during tough negotiations.

As a strengthened ally, you are learning to use cognitive-behavioral therapy along with your loved one. Your role consists of supporting and encouraging the completion of the assignments without nagging or becoming overly involved. If your loved one is unable to finish them, it will be discussed in session as part of the therapeutic process.

Therapy is often a two-steps-forward-one-step-back proposition. During this challenging time of confronting old, destructive patterns of thinking and learning new ways to cope, your role as strengthened ally is critical. As your loved one begins to make progress in his therapy, validate and applaud his little victories, as well as your own. Sometimes healing comes in baby steps, but it is healing, nonetheless.

◆

CHAPTER 7

Drug Therapies

DEPRESSION IS NOT A SIGN OF YOUR LOVED ONE'S weakness or a character flaw. It's a *bona fide* medical diagnosis like diabetes or heart disease that, when severe enough, requires medical attention. And, just like diabetes or heart disease, if it is undertreated or left untreated, depression can worsen and may even have permanent impact on the body (the brain, in this case) with life-threatening consequences such as suicide attempts. Research now shows that most episodes of untreated depression last for six months to two years and often recur. That's the bad news—particularly because depression causes so much loss and pain for everyone involved. But it doesn't have to be that way.

Today there is a bigger repertoire of options than ever for effectively treating and even curing depression. And research is continuing to discover which medications in what combinations taken for how many months are the most effective for which patients (see Chapter 8). We still don't know why it can take six weeks before your loved one begins feeling better or why some antidepressants work for some people but not for others, but we do know that for 90 percent of those who take some combination of medications they work at least to some degree. Seventy percent of patients who have had only one episode of depression recover fully. So there is much to be hopeful about.

But before we jump into a discussion of particular drugs, I'd like you to think about what's being called the *5 Rs of Antidepressant Treatment.* This will help you understand what to expect as your loved one embarks on a course of treatment and will also give you some background when talking with your loved one's caregiving team.

THE 5 Rs OF TREATMENT WITH ANTIDEPRESSANTS

- *Response:* This means your loved one is experiencing a 50 percent reduction in his symptoms. Perhaps his mood has improved or he feels more energetic. However, he's still not back to his old self.
- *Remission:* The symptoms have disappeared! Your loved one feels entirely better and can resume his old life with zest. He is well.
- *Recovery:* Your loved one has been in remission for six to twelve months and is ready to meet the world head-on.

- *Relapse:* Your loved one's symptoms, although better for a while, have now worsened before he reached remission or recovery.
- *Recurrence:* The symptoms return a few months after your loved one has experienced recovery.

Today, research has shown that treatment with antidepressant medications is highly effective. About two-thirds of depressed individuals respond to this kind of therapy and about 90 percent or more may respond over time to a combination of antidepressant medications if they stick to their drug regimen. (See Chapter 8.) The shame is that only a third of those who could benefit from drug therapy ever avail themselves of it. (This low number is due to a variety of factors including the stigma that's still attached to obtaining mental health treatment and inadequate resources.)

WHEN SHOULD DRUG THERAPY BE SOUGHT?

The most common and effective treatment for severely depressed individuals is a combination of psychotherapy and antidepressant medication. These two approaches reinforce each other—the psychotherapy puts your loved one in a frame of mind in which he is more apt to stick to the medication schedule, and the medication puts him in the frame of mind in which his therapy is more apt to be beneficial. Overall, it's a win-win situation. And recent research has shown that although medications and psychotherapy travel different pathways in the brain, they both positively affect the same area.

According to the latest guidelines of the American Psychiatric Association, patients with mild to moderate depression can benefit from psychotherapy alone. However, if symptoms persist for more than twenty sessions or worsen during that time, or if the depression is diagnosed as moderate to severe, medication is recommended.

I will refer a depressed patient to a psychopharmacologist for an evaluation and potential medical treatment if he:

- has suffered repeated bouts of depression in the past
- has a family history of the disorder
- continues to struggle with negative thoughts, hopelessness, and despair after six to ten weeks of psychotherapy—that is, the Cognitive Behavioral Therapy is having only a limited effect.

HOW DRUG THERAPIES WORK

Many myths persist surrounding the use of antidepressant medications—that they are addictive, that they are uppers, that they rob one of independence, that they make you a different person, or that you will not be able to feel naturally anymore. Perhaps these and other anxieties have sprung from the way depression was treated in the 1950s and '60s, with addictive tranquilizers such as Valium that masked symptoms rather than treating them.

But today's antidepressants are neither tranquilizers nor "uppers," nor are they addictive. They are a distinct group of medications that work specifically on brain chemistry to mitigate the underlying causes of the illness.

Imbalances in certain brain chemicals called neurotransmitters (especially serotonin, dopamine, and norepinephrine) are thought to trigger depression. Neurotransmitters are chemicals that the nerve cells themselves create and release to communicate with each other. They are essential for sending messages from one nerve cell to another.

With the help of Magnetic Resonance Imaging (MRI) scans, researchers are beginning to understand how this works. They now know, for example, that nerve cells pump out and are continually awash in a bath of neurotransmitters. They attach themselves or "bind" to receptors on neighboring cells (much like a key fits into a lock) in order to send their message to the receiving cell. Some neurotransmitters excite nerve cells to action while others diminish activity. Once the message is sent, the neurotransmitters return to the nerve cell of origin or they're broken down chemically.

Each neurotransmitter has specific receptors to which it will attach (again, like a lock and key) on the adjacent cell. And each nerve cell can have thousands of neuroreceptors to accommodate a wide variety of neurotransmitters. (Some theories about why it takes a person so long to feel better once on antidepressants suggest that it takes time for these neuroreceptors to "upregulate" their numbers to be able to make better contact with the increased serotonin, which itself may happen in a matter of days.)

Researchers believe that diminished levels of neurotransmitters and neuroreceptors cause the sleep problems, irritability, anxiety, fatigue, diet disruptions, and despondent mood that underlie depression. For instance, norepinephrine regulates alertness and arousal. Decreased levels in certain areas of the brain may contribute to the fatigue and depressed mood of the illness.

And lowered serotonin activity may be linked to impulsiveness, aggression, violence, and suicidal behavior. Autopsies of people who have committed suicide have revealed less serotonin in the fluid surrounding the brain and spinal cord than normal; and brain cells in an area of the brain called the frontal cortex in these people seem to have more receptors for serotonin, as if to make up for the inadequate supply. By contrast, other studies have associated high levels of serotonin with leadership behaviors.

Brain imaging such as MRIs and PET scans have also shown less activity in an area of the prefrontal cortex of individuals with depression. The prefrontal cortex is a specific area of the brain just behind the eyes. This structure, part of what's called our "executive function area," organizes and prioritizes the flow of information through the cortex. It is the seat of our ability to hold newly acquired bits of information and interrelate them with what we already know. It allows us to understand spoken language as well as accomplish tasks in which we must remember visual images that are no longer in view. It's also an area important in organizing emotional responses to socially significant or provocative situations.

This vital area seems to be much smaller than average in individuals who suffer from depression and bipolar illness, although scientists are still unsure whether this abnormality is the cause or the result of the illness. However, researchers believe that it is not just decreased activity in one area of the brain that influences mood disorders, but that other areas of the brain are also involved. The neurotransmitters are produced in many parts of the brain and travel to the areas where they have their effect.

The goal of most antidepressants, then, is to increase the amount of neurotransmitters in the brain. Medications like Prozac, Zoloft, Celexa, and Lexapro—also known as SSRIs, or selective serotonin reuptake inhibitors—block the body's reabsorption of serotonin, allowing more to circulate in the bloodstream. Other newer medications such as Cymbalta and Effexor increase norepinephrine in addition to serotonin, but they do so through different mechanisms (touching on different receptors) than, say, Zoloft.

As antidepressants relieve pessimistic, suicidal thoughts, they can also alleviate the other symptoms—insomnia, anxiety, sensitivity to rejection, and lethargy—that accompany your loved one's depression. They also increase vitality, focus, purpose, and socialization. Disappointment is better managed in a more measured way. Medications can be combined and may work synergistically—each boosting the effectiveness of the other.

DRUG TREATMENT

Antidepressant drugs are often prescribed by psychiatrists, who are physicians. I recommend this course of action. However, because of the stigma attached to mental health treatment, depressed individuals often receive prescriptions for antidepressants from their primary care physicians. This may be adequate and appropriate for people with mild depression or those who wouldn't get treatment elsewhere. However, if your loved one gets antidepressants from your family doctor, the illness may not be monitored closely enough and symptoms and subtle side effects may not be treated adequately. And this, in turn, can lead to the risk of your loved one going off the medication or not getting the full benefit of the treatment. In addition, medical treatment of depression by primary care physicians often does not include the important support of psychotherapy.

If your loved one is seeing a psychologist, social worker, or family therapist for psychotherapy, that individual will refer him to a psychiatrist, psychopharmacologist, or biopsychiatrist for evaluation and possible treatment. The physician will work hand in hand with your loved one's therapist to monitor his progress and response.

The psychiatrist should order a thorough physical, including a neurological exam and some laboratory tests, to determine

- any physiological causes for the depression
- evidence of substance abuse
- liver, heart, and thyroid function
- the best possible treatments

He or she will also see your loved one on a regular basis—usually monthly but sometimes weekly—to monitor blood levels and the efficacy of the medications. You'll find guidelines for what to look for in a good psychiatrist in Chapter 11.

There is no way to predict which medication will be most effective; some individuals respond well to one drug but not at all to another. And some respond to a combination of medications that work synergistically with each other. As Mark S. Gold explains in *The Good News About Depression,* "Depression seem[s] to be not one but several illnesses that share a common symptom constellation. . . . Depression has several subtypes. As a rule, each subtype responds to treatment with a certain kind of antidepressant. . . . The standard of care is that there is *no one* standard of care." Unfortunately we do not yet have the tests that would enable us to identify those subtypes on a routine basis. That's what can make the medical treatment of depression so demanding, time consuming, and frustrating, especially when the first line of treatment appears to not work (see Chapter 8 for a more detailed discussion of resistant depression).

Despite my earlier analogy, however, depression is not exactly like diabetes, which has a specific treatment protocol. The procedure for dealing with depression is as singular as your loved one's fingerprint.

The doctor may proceed by trial and error until a satisfactory treatment is found. Sometimes complex tests are performed to detect neurotransmitters, enzymes, and hormones associated with depression in order to zero in on the proper treatment plan with as little delay as possible. Persistence, flexibility, and patience are key.

Once treatment starts, usually the first sign that the medication is working appears in a week or two as insomnia begins to subside. Despair abates; anxiety and reactivity are quieted. Other symptoms diminish over the next several weeks, but it can take six weeks at each dosage level until you see a strong response and even longer for remission.

A thirty-six-year-old musician, Jeremy, had a depression that was complicated by intense anxiety. The course of his treatment is typical of many people I've seen. At first he was put on a low dose of an antidepressant coupled with an equally low dose of an anti-anxiety medication. After several weeks, it was clear that this regime was not having the hoped-for effect. Going back to the drawing board, his psychiatrist changed the antianxiety drug. A month or so later, there still was not much change. Then, the doctor increased its dosage while maintaining the antidepressant dosage. This finally worked.

Jeremy felt calmer and more buoyant than he had in years. The difference was significant. In fact, he was surprised at how much better he felt. But it took a total of four and a half months to get it right. Each person is different, and part of the role of psychotherapy is finding a balance between changing medications and staying the course. And this is where your role as a strengthened ally becomes particularly important, including reassuring your loved one and making it clear that you will get through this together (see Chapters 4 and 5).

Even after the depression lifts (which can take six weeks or more), your loved one's psychiatrist may keep him on the drug for twelve months or longer, especially if there has been a family history of depression, to ensure that there is no relapse or recurrence. In cases where there have been three or more episodes of depression in a lifetime, relapses are more likely, and medication may be required as part of regular long-term treatment.

As with all drugs, there is also the possibility of side effects such as weight gain or loss, rashes, dry mouth, sedation, insomnia, agitation, palpitations, sexual dysfunction, or stomach upset. Sometimes these appear soon after treatment begins, but weeks before the symptoms of depression abate. If severe, the side effects might interfere with your loved one's willingness to continue treatment. For further discussion of adherence problems, see page 137. The caregiving team will watch for signs of side effects and may change or add medications or may adjust the dosage if the prescribed one seems to have little effect or if the side effects seem intolerable. Many of these side effects do, however, disappear over time.

It can take several weeks for a medication to reach the proper level in the bloodstream—called the therapeutic dosage—before it becomes fully effective. This can vary greatly from individual to individual. Older people, for example, metabolize these medications much more slowly, and consequently it takes less time for the therapeutic dosage to accumulate. Therefore older people often require smaller doses than young adults. The search for the proper dosage can be a tricky business that takes some time and expertise.

Sometimes, choosing an antidepressant that can address more than the depressive symptoms can be helpful. According to Dr. Andrew Roth, a psychiatrist at Memorial Sloan Kettering Hospital in Manhattan, "Selecting a calming medication for someone with anxiety or insomnia is helpful. Or opting for an energizing medicine for someone who has a lethargic type of depression may be beneficial. The psychiatrist may want to add additional medications to achieve these purposes more quickly. The addition of a medication to specifically address anxiety or sleep (such as Ativan, Klonopin, or Ambien) can give the depressed person significant relief within hours to days as he waits for the antidepressant to kick in, which may take weeks."

As difficult as waiting may be, when someone you love is depressed, maintaining hope and patience is part of being a strengthened ally. Let's take a look at some of these medications in more detail.

SSRI ANTIDEPRESSANTS

SSRIs such as Prozac, Celexa, Lexapro, Paxil, and Zoloft have been hailed as a breakthrough in the treatment of depression, since they seem to act more quickly than the older tricyclic medications, and people who take them report fewer side effects. This makes them easier to tolerate. In addition, since they seem to be less interactive with other medications, they are often prescribed to elderly or medically ill patients, who may be suffering from other conditions that require drug therapy.

However, side effects do exist. These could include sexual dysfunction (reduced desire and/or ability to achieve orgasm), gastrointestinal distress, decreased appetite, agitation, or insomnia. Weight gain and the feeling of being sedated are rare. For many individuals, these side effects are minimal and go away with time. If your loved one experiences discomfort with one medication, there are others that may be just as effective or even more so without these consequences.

TRICYCLIC ANTIDEPRESSANTS

The word "tricyclic" refers to the chemical structure of the medication and not its effect. This group includes the drugs Tofranil, Elavil, Norpramin, Pamelor, Aventyl, and Ludiomil.

Tricyclic antidepressants primarily block the absorption or reuptake of the neurotransmitter norepinephrine, which acts in the brain to regulate anxiety and panic and also serotonin. Elavil and Tofranil are two of the original medications in this class. They are also prescribed for anxiety, insomnia, and chronic pain.

Side effects can occur with all tricyclic antidepressants. These include drowsiness, dry mouth, blurry vision, constipation, decreased sexual desire, difficulty urinating, increased or irregular heart rate, memory loss, and dizziness, which at therapeutic doses can make it difficult to stay on the medication. These medications may present special difficulties for the elderly, as dizziness and other side effects can lead to falls. Your loved one should ask his psychiatrist for strategies to counteract some of these discomforts. For example, when tricyclics are taken at bedtime, many of the side effects will occur while your loved one is sleeping.

DOPAMINE-NOREPINEPHRINE REUPTAKE INHIBITORS

This class of drugs includes medications such as Wellbutrin and Zyban (used for smoking cessation). These medications boost the neurotransmitters dopamine and norepinephrine in the brain. It gives individuals an energy boost in the morning and is available in immediate, sustained, and timed release form. Dry mouth, constipation, nausea, weight loss, insomnia, dizziness, headache, and agitation are potential side effects. These medications are not recommended for people who have histories of seizure disorder or bulimia.

MONOAMINE OXIDASE INHIBITOR ANTIDEPRESSANTS (MAOIs)

MAOIs include the medications Marplan, Nardil, and Parnate. These are thought to operate by retarding the breakdown of neurotransmitters called monoamines in the brain. These are the chemicals the brain uses to reabsorb neurotransmitters like serotonin and norepinephrine. Decreased levels of monoamines have been associated with suicide and, in people with bipolar disorder, with thrill seeking and impulsiveness.

Although MAOIs can be quite effective, they are not without risks. The same monoamines that exist in the brain also occur in other parts of the body, including the intestines. Certain foods contain large amounts of monoamines as well. Individuals taking MAOIs may absorb too much of this substance, leading to high blood pressure and even strokes and death. These side effects are of particular concern to the elderly and those with medical or pain conditions for which they are already taking other medications that may interact with the MAOI.

In order to avoid this danger, those who take MAOIs must avoid the following foodstuffs (the prescribing physician will provide specific instructions about dietary restrictions, which must be carefully adhered to):

- aged cheeses like Parmesan, Swiss, or cheddar (cottage and cream cheese are safe)
- yogurt

- pickled, smoked, or fermented meats such as herring, lox, dried sausage, hard salami, or beef jerky
- liver
- lima, fava, Chinese, or English beans
- more than one glass of beer, wine, or sherry (Chianti is dangerous)
- large amounts of caffeine (including that in sodas) or chocolate
- canned figs
- Marmite, Bovril, or other yeast or meat extracts (these may be hidden in soups and stews).

However, a new form of MAOI, Emsam, available as a skin patch, can eliminate the need for these food restrictions, especially if given in small doses (nine mgs. or less).

Another risk factor is that other medications, including those that can be purchased over the counter, may interact with MAOIs. Your loved one's psychiatrist should be fully informed of *any* medications your loved one is taking while on MAOIs. For instance, aspirin and Tylenol are safe, as long as they are not taken as a component of cold preparations, such as Co-Tylenol. And, SSRIs can be dangerous when taken in combination with MAOIs.

Because of MAOIs' potential to cause stroke and death, a severely depressed individual can use them to attempt suicide by taking an overdose, or by combining them with alcohol and/or dangerous foods.

OTHER ANTIDEPRESSANTS

Cymbalta and Effexor are dual-mechanism drugs that boost serotonin and norepinephrine. Cymbalta is also used to treat anxiety coupled with depression and pain, especially pain from nerve damage due to diabetes. It is a bit more sedating than Zoloft (so might be useful for someone suffering from insomnia), and it decreases appetite (and thus may be helpful for someone who has been overeating as a result of the depression). In addition to depression, Effexor is recommended for anxiety and panic and can also be used for post-traumatic stress disorder and severe PMS.

Remeron also works on norepinephrine and serotonin, blocking the reuptake of these neurotransmitters in different ways than the typical SSRIs. Because it has a calming effect, it is useful for those suffering from insomnia or anxiety related to their depression. This is the only antidepressant without gastric upset. However, unwanted weight gain and daytime sedation may be common with this drug.

LITHIUM

Drugs most often used in manic-depressive illness are called mood stabilizers and they ease the uncontrolled highs of mania. Lithium, the most commonly prescribed mood stabilizer, not only treats acute episodes of mania but also helps to prevent future occurrences. It can even treat the depressive phase of bipolar illness. Sometimes anticonvulsive drugs such as Depakote are also prescribed. Contrary to generally held beliefs, these medications are not addictive. They are corrective—that is, they repair a neurochemical imbalance.

Lithium is effective in stabilizing moods and preventing the recurrence of manic or depressive episodes. It works well in 60 to 70 percent of bipolar patients and takes less than a week to become effective. Although scientists have not yet determined exactly how it works, it is thought that lithium also impacts the neurotransmitters in the brain.

Side effects can include excessive thirst, urinary problems, lack of coordination, tremors, nausea and vomiting, and tiredness.

Lithium may also be prescribed to an individual who is suffering from depression, as an adjunct to other medications.

Those individuals who experience rapid cycling bipolar illness seem to do better on Tegretol, a drug also used successfully for epilepsy.

YOUR ROLE AS A STRENGTHENED ALLY

While you may believe that your loved one's success with medications is entirely in the hands of his psychiatrist and the medications themselves, you can play a very important role in the recovery process.

As you've seen, it may take many weeks for your loved one to begin feeling the full effect of the prescribed antidepressant he is taking. However, according to Los Angeles psychiatrist Christine Forest, many patients with depression don't recognize or report the tiny "micro-improvements" that can occur for weeks along the way.

"Maybe the patient has a little more energy or he's sleeping a little less," she explained to me. "Maybe his appetite has improved a bit or he went to the market for the first time in two years. Maybe she cooked a meal or bought some yarn for needlepoint or started reading a novel. The family will observe these micro-improvements first, even if the patient does not."

In your role as strengthened ally, it is incredibly valuable for you to illuminate and describe to your loved one these essential small steps toward improvement. Watch for signs. Most patients are eager to get well and can become discouraged if it takes a long time for the medications to kick in. They may even abandon treatment before giving the antidepressants the weeks it takes to be fully effective. But your belief that your loved one can—and indeed, *is* getting better—will help him keep going. Your hopefulness provides support.

In fact, even if your loved one does not report any improvement, or if these micro-moments don't register with her, you can stick to the "facts." "I noticed that you had an easier time getting up in the morning," you might say. Or, "You really enjoyed the children's visit today." Do not necessarily expect your loved one to agree with you. Just underscore the facts and what you observe without demanding your loved one's acquiescence. In fact, she may disagree or say, "That's nothing compared to how badly I feel."

Your best response is, "I know it is hard to see the little improvements. But I feel these will add up to something more. I believe they will and I am glad to share them with you." Sometimes charting with your loved one these improvements in activities, mood, sleep, and appetite over time can help her appreciate the overall direction of recovery, even if there are occasional setbacks or plateaus.

Be thoughtful. Don't get hung up on what your loved one is feeling or you may end up going down the same negative spiral. Keep your focus on observed behaviors. Anchor your loved one's progress in concrete, tangible improvements that she can think about and maximize. Listen for indicators of better functioning and better decision-making and point them out. Ultimately, your message will be, "You can get better. You are getting better. Keep on going. I'm with you all the way!"

ADHERENCE

As your loved one's mood begins to brighten, you or he may think he no longer needs the medication. This is a mistake. It's vital that he continues to take the antidepressant as prescribed in order to maintain a therapeutic dose, not just when he feels depressed. The drug's effectiveness depends upon its regular use and the attainment of consistent levels of the medication in the blood.

My patient Mike did well on Prozac, but after six months on the drug, he found himself experiencing some pressure from other family members to "kick his habit" and "make it on his own." To some of them, Mike's taking Prozac was the same as his marijuana use; it indicated a lack of resolve. They saw it as a personal weakness.

Under such scrutiny and persistent pressure, Mike reluctantly acquiesced, thinking, "Why not give it a try?" He took a break from medication. The results were crushing. Within a week he was finding it difficult to get out of bed. He became distracted and withdrawn. When we discussed this rapid change for the worse, Mike truly began to face the importance of his medication and the neurobiological elements of depression. From that point on, when talking with his family he used the analogy of a diabetic needing insulin.

Challenges to adherence—not following doctors' orders, particularly in regard to taking medication—can be a feature of depression. You, as a strengthened ally, play an important supportive role in managing this issue. Non-adherence can start from good intentions: "I don't need so much medication; I'm feeling better." Or the reverse, "If one pill makes me feel so good, maybe if I take more, I'll feel better sooner." Unfortunately, such an attitude can slow recovery. It can also place an undue burden on you if you are called upon to put the pieces together when your loved one's untreated, undertreated, or overtreated depression creates distress, confusion, and despair. Dealing with your loved one's adherence issues is one of the difficulties you face when someone you love is depressed.

Why do people ignore their physician's prescriptions and recommendations? In *An Unquiet Mind*, the psychologist Kay Redfield Jamison writes extensively about her resistance to taking lithium. It was fueled less by the side effects—the loss of coordination, the difficulty reading, the memory lapses—that she experienced while on the drug than by the longing for the highs of her manic periods, which seemed to give her life so much color; now, in their absence, her existence was rendered dull.

Jamison notes that it's hard for those with bipolar illness to relinquish "the positive aspects of the illness that can arise during the milder manic states: heightened energy and perceptual awareness, increased fluidity and originality of thinking, intense exhilaration of moods and experience, increased sexual desire, expansiveness of vision, and a lengthened grasp of aspiration. . . . These intoxicating experiences were highly addictive in nature and difficult to give up."

No wonder she resisted taking the medication, like many others suffering from manic-depressive illness. Who would want to forgo such a good time? That these high times were followed by terrible lows seemed inconsequential when the manic phase was in full swing.

Eventually, however, it became clear to Jamison that the havoc her noncompliance engendered for her family and loved ones (including the heavy financial burden caused by a credit-card spending spree during a manic episode) far outweighed the exhilaration she experienced. She had to face the fact that the ultimate responsibility for her cure depended on her compliance with medication protocols. Her partnership with her treating physician became crucial to her successful treatment.

There are other reasons for noncompliance. Medication is an everyday reminder to your loved one that he is ill. There is a longing to believe that he is better. In a paradoxical way, lack of adherence seems hopeful. Moreover, the depression itself can in some ways work against an individual's following a prescribed course of treatment. The hopelessness inherent in depression may lead your loved one to believe that the medication won't help him or that it's useless to try any therapy. The depression may also cause him to become forgetful. He may not remember whether or when he took his last dose of medication, and may then compensate by taking too much or too little.

As mentioned earlier, individuals on drug therapy may also stop taking their medication because they are feeling better and believe they no longer need it or because of uncomfortable side effects. Lack of adherence can also take the form of creative self-medication. Some individuals increase their dosage or supplement with leftovers from old prescriptions without their doctor's knowledge or approval, reasoning that if some antidepressant makes them feel good, more will help them feel even better. Or patients start and stop as their moods shift, not understanding that they need to maintain an appropriate therapeutic dosage in the blood at all times for the medication to be effective.

One of the more common side effects of SSRIs and other medications is reduced sexual desire or, in men, erectile dysfunction. This can also tempt one into noncompliance, and is an important issue to discuss with your loved one's psychiatrist. Antidepressants such as Wellbutrin and Remeron may have far fewer sexual side effects than other antidepressants, or in some cases erection enhancing medications (under the physician's supervision) such as Viagra, Cialis, and Levitra may be prescribed to counter the sexual side effects of the patient's medication.

According to biopsychiatrist Mark S. Gold, 20 to 25 percent of all hospital admissions for depression result from lack of adherence. "Family members can help immeasurably," he writes, "by encouraging compliance with the doctor's orders and by keeping track."

Lack of adherence is like a warning sign on the freeway, telling you to proceed with caution. It can be managed if you are attentive.

However, sometimes even the most compliant patient does not get better. What happens if your loved one's depression seems to hang on like a rusty nail that refuses to budge? In the next chapter, we'll look at what to do if your loved one is suffering from what I call "resistant depression."

◆

Dealing with Resistant Depression

CLAIRE HAD BEEN IN MY CARE SINCE SHE WAS A teenager. She had been plagued by constant self-doubt, including feelings that her friends really didn't like her—irrespective of her talents, good humor, and generous nature. When I first saw her, she had already attempted suicide twice. Her parents were frantic, and terrified that with the next attempt she might be successful in ending her life. Despite short stints on medication and weekly therapy with other therapists, nothing seemed to work.

When I first met with Claire, I gently probed her about what had motivated the suicide attempts. "I just didn't want to have to be in pain all the time," she told me. "The last time, I had stepped on one of my CDs and cracked the case. That just sent me over the edge. It felt like one more failure to me, and I couldn't take it anymore." I asked her whether anything else had happened—any other stressors, challenges, or disappointments that had occurred prior to the attempt.

She sat quietly, head slumped forward for a several minutes and finally added softly, "I backed my car into a pole that afternoon. I was so anxious because I had three exams to study for, and it takes me so much longer than my friends to focus and read the assignments."

The fact that seemingly insignificant incidents like breaking a CD case or a fender-bender could result in such despair and such a risky act was upsetting to everyone. But it also gave us a glimpse into Claire's distress and pain. Impulsivity when triggered is a potentially lethal risk in a depressed teenager or adult, and in Claire's case needed to be addressed immediately. Just imagine for a moment what it would feel like in your inner world if what makes you feel good about yourself disappeared in an instant, giving the sense that nothing pleasurable and positive lasts. Just imagine the difficulty of holding onto hope if you found yourself in this situation. It can be so comforting for a loved one who is depressed if his or her strengthened ally understands this experience. It helps the depressed person feel less alone and abandoned.

It also seemed to me that Claire wasn't able to derive satisfaction from her accomplishments. Despite the fact that she was an A student, an excellent swimmer, and had many friends, she still felt like a failure. I started assessing her other symptoms. Was there a distractibility problem? Was there underlying anxiety? What was the family history around depression and anxiety?

I assembled a team to get a fresh look at all of my young

patient's symptoms and problems. The team included Claire herself, her parents, a psychopharmacologist, and a second psychiatrist who was expert in adolescent issues. The latter we brought in as consultant to help with the assessment. Together, the team reviewed Claire's school records and conducted psychological testing.

We learned that Claire was suffering from Attention Deficit Disorder (ADD) which would account for some of the impulsivity we'd seen as well as her distractibility in finishing school assignments. We also diagnosed social anxiety and severe depression accompanied by a profound sense of hopelessness. This was exemplified by a harshly critical inner voice that put a negative spin on nearly every social interaction and accomplishment. We discovered that other family members—a grandmother on each side of her family and an aunt—also suffered from depression. These factors meant that she might have a genetic disposition to the illness.

As I undertook building a trusting and supportive therapeutic relationship with Claire and began to engage her in cognitive behavioral therapy, the psychiatrists outlined a strategy for antidepressant and antianxiety medications. Unlike the relatively quick successes I've seen with many other patients, this was an arduous process. Claire went through a whole sequence of medications that made her either too sleepy or too agitated.

What does that really mean for a teenager? Well, if you're foggy or jumpy in class, teachers react, questioning your behavior, motivation, or performance. They may ask embarrassing questions in front of your classmates: "What's wrong with you—weren't you listening?" The last thing Claire wanted was for anyone at school to know that she was depressed or taking medication. So she would lie: "I haven't been sleeping well." These excuses would only go so far, though, and school became even more stressful for her.

We experimented with dosages—was she taking too much? Too little? The wrong medication? We followed a stepwise progression, literally experimenting by trial and error with feedback from Claire. However, since these medications take several weeks to reach the therapeutic dosage, my patient was still depressed and wasn't always a reliable "reporter." We also asked her parents if they'd observed any changes. Trust is essential in a therapeutic relationship, and having to include Claire's parents made her suspicious at times. "Why do you have to talk to them?" she asked me. "Don't you believe me?" We had to find a balance between privacy and confidentiality on the one hand, and treatment and family support on the other, in order to determine what medications in which doses were the most effective, with the fewest side effects. It was hard, frustrating work for everyone, but we persisted and persevered.

I've walked you through the actual experience of one patient in some detail so you can work with yourself to manage your longing to have results in face of a depression that is seemingly resistant to treatment. This case and many like it continue to be a challenge for patients and their families, and this is true not only because of the dangerous nature of severe depression. Indeed, as you may well know, life doesn't stand idly by as we work on the illness. It has a way of throwing us surprises while in the midst of treatment—in Claire's case, a rejection letter from her first-choice college, a conflict with her teacher, a hurtful offhand remark from her boyfriend—all of which increase the risk of despair returning. Yes, that's right. Claire had a boyfriend, but she was suspicious of him as well—"He's just saying I'm pretty so I'll be intimate with him," she complained. But nevertheless, one step at a time, we slowly found a way through.

It took nearly a year to see any progress. In fact, the most difficult part of this stage of treatment was for Claire to hold onto micro-improvements in the face of her hopelessness. And what did those improvements look like? Here's a typical example: She went from being nearly suicidal every day to the new thought: "It would be okay if I got hit by a car and died or if I died in a drive-by shooting, but I wouldn't want to have it on my parents' head that I killed myself." Even though it was hard for Claire to think of this as a step forward, we had to appreciate it as progress. It was a tiny shift in attitude, but it was significant nonetheless.

Claire's is but one example of a whole group of teens and adults who suffer from a seemingly resistant depression that takes patience and perseverance to treat. Some patients may even need to be hospitalized in order to create a safe enough environment for psychotherapy and medication to relieve the suffering and diminish the risk of suicide. If your loved one is in this situation, I counsel you to maintain hope.

MANAGING EXPECTATIONS: ON OPTIMISM AND HOPE

One of the most challenging aspects of dealing with resistant depression is managing expectations—yours as a caregiver and strengthened ally as well as your loved one's—in regard to treatments and remission. And so, before I go into a more complete explanation of the strategies that are currently being used to treat resistant depression, I want you to understand the difference between optimism and hope.

Jerome Groopman, M.D., author of *The Anatomy of Hope,* explains that a positive attitude or optimism is the thought: "Everything is going to turn out for the best." But as you may well know, life isn't like that. Sometimes bad things happen to wonderful people—and things don't turn out for the best, despite your best intentions and efforts.

Hope, in contrast, does not make that assumption. Rather, in a clear-eyed manner, a person with hope assesses all the problems, challenges, or obstacles, and through information and education seeks and finds a possible *realistic* path to a better future. This future is often unknown and unknowable but is constantly reassessed based upon new information. A person with true hope will experience a wide range of emotions including fear, relief, joy, anger, and sadness. Yet through it all, he or she will try to move forward despite the ups and downs.

I cannot overemphasize the importance of keeping yourself well informed about the latest research on treating resistant depressions, as this will help you and your loved one maintain hope even as you manage your expectations. In the Appendix is a list of Web sites that provide the latest research and information on new discoveries in treating depression. Please consider consulting these sites often as well as looking for new sources of support and information.

In Chapter 2, I described depression to you as a biopsychosocial illness. Fundamentally, treatment for resistant depression requires us to manage two components: the psychology of depression, which we treat on the psychosocial front with cognitive-behavioral therapy (see Chapter 6) and the underlying biology, which we address through psychopharmacology (see the previous chapter and below). In this chapter, I will first address treatments from a psychological perspective, and then we'll look at the latest research in medical interventions.

THE PSYCHOLOGY OF DEPRESSION:
REINING IN THE FOUR HORSEMEN
OF THE APOCALYPSE

For years, I have been working within a cognitive-behavioral framework that my patients report as particularly useful and meaningful, especially when they have the kind of depression that Claire suffered from, which seems resistant to treatment.

I call it *depression-as-thought,* and it is composed of four elements. I visualize them as The Four Horsemen of the Apocalypse:

- self-abnegation
- personalization
- immobility
- inertia

In order for us to work in this framework, I explain several assumptions to my patient with depression. First, depression-as-thought is like a voice in his head talking to him all the time. Second, this voice is not *him* although he may think that it defines who he is. Third, this voice and its litany of criticism must be challenged. Fourth, the voice functions because the chatter has *just enough truth* to it to make him believe that what it's saying is *completely* true. Remember, though, that *just enough truth* is not the same as *complete truth*. Fifth, the voice functions to undermine his will—an essential ingredient in treating depression through cognitive-behavioral therapy. Finally, depression-as-thought morphs—changes its tack if he challenges it—making it all the more difficult to rein in. That said, the four horsemen of depression include:

Self-abnegation refers to self-criticism—that persistent negative voice that prevents one from deriving satisfaction from one's accomplishments or efforts. It's the voice of doom and gloom that sabotages every decision and action with, "Yes, but . . ." This kind of self-criticism leads many patients to talk about shattered goals, being cursed, or living under a perpetual dark cloud. Pernicious as they are, such negative thoughts keep a person stuck in his depression by preventing him from experiencing any joy and reinforcing a sense of powerlessness and hopelessness. He lives with a pervasive sense that "No matter what I do, I'll never be any good; nothing ever works out for me."

Personalization is a different kind of negative thought pattern. A person who personalizes takes offense at the slightest infraction. When the parking lot attendant fails to smile while handing over the claim ticket, Jennifer thinks the attendant is being rude and reacts angrily although there is no reason to believe his behavior is personal. Or if the bank teller doesn't thank her after a transaction, she feels slighted—and reacts as if utterly rejected. A friend doesn't notice that she got a haircut, and ends up in the dog house.

A person with depression can globalize these incidents, blowing them all out of proportion. She may explode over something that seems insignificant to you, but that rage can later turn to a litany of prior offenses and hurts—repeating like a mantra all the emotional experiences since childhood that a given incident triggers. Others may be thrown off balance for a whole day. Reactions such as these can lead you to feel as if you're constantly walking in a minefield, never knowing what will ignite the fireworks.

Personalization distracts your loved one from staying focused on what's important. She may find herself blaming others for her own inability to take action, when this lack of action is a common result of self-abnegation and personalization.

Taken together, these two thought patterns result in the behavioral patterns of immobility and inertia that perpetuate depression in a vicious cycle.

Immobility is the inability to start any activity—the difficulty of kicking into gear. It's as if your loved one who is depressed walks up to the starting line and then just stands there, stuck. He just can't take that first step. Although he may know what to do, he doesn't do it. The depression-as-thought introduces just enough doubt to prevent action. My patients describe their lives moving in slow motion. They will find themselves distracted by a thought or a memory and lose focus or direction. They find themselves feeling tired although they've rested. Some speak about it as lethargy or just losing time, like the day is wasting away.

This is frustrating for you as a strengthened ally because you know in your heart that if your loved one would just act, he would feel better. Even he knows that, but it seems to make no difference! That's what makes depression-as-thought so challenging. In order to activate will, a person must derive satisfaction from his accomplishments. But, as we saw with Claire, this feeling is absent because of the self-abnegating voice harping on what hasn't yet been accomplished, or introducing potential problems that thwart forward movement.

How does one derive satisfaction from accomplishments in order to become mobilized? This is a slow process in which the focus is on behaviors and efforts, not outcomes. Activating will requires constant reframing of thoughts. But the good news is that many of my patients report that once they become engaged in catching their thoughts and managing the dismissive voice, they can actually experience a sense of satisfaction and accomplishment.

Inertia refers to the experience of time disappearing when one is in thought. Your loved one escapes, tunes out, or seems lost in a brain fog. He knows what to do but can't make himself move. He can't even get out of bed. It's as if any effort is like slogging through molasses. It takes forever to clean an apartment, cook a meal, complete an assignment.

THE MORPHING OF DEPRESSION-AS-THOUGHT

Part of the challenge with depression is that once you've mastered a specific goal, the success does not easily generalize to the next goal. Remember the depressed individual's painful challenge of deriving satisfaction from his accomplishments? Well in resistant depressions, self-esteem does not build from previous successes. It's as if your loved one is starting from zero with each new undertaking.

I call this depression-as-thought *morphing* itself. Why morphing? I got the idea from watching too many science fiction movies—in particular *The Terminator* and *The Matrix* series. Consider how the computer-generated "enemy" in these films changes personalities or quickly transforms into another entity in order to confuse the hero and succeed in its destructive mission. The same can be said for depression-as-thought. It morphs in order to prevent your loved one from feeling good about his steady progress. When your loved one manages negative thoughts in one arena, and he actually does show some improvement, those destructive thoughts switch to some other self-defeating target. Here are some examples:

• Allison was able to overcome her immobility and inertia and actually found a way to join a support group. Soon, though, she found herself thinking: "This group is fine, but it's not for me. The people aren't like me at all; their problems are much easier to manage. I'm going to quit." Even though she took the positive action of finding and joining the group, she later minimized its helpfulness.

- Jon submitted a job resume but then focused on his lack of qualifications, "Why would they want me?" he asked himself, thereby sabotaging the interview before it even started.

- After several months of battling depression, Kevin finally agreed that it would be worthwhile to see a psychophar-macologist. He met with the psychiatrist, who prescribed medication. This appeared hopeful, but in the very next session he blamed his passivity—"I really didn't do any-thing. I'm like a sheep following your orders. Go here, go there, do this . . . do that!"

The morphing of depression-as-thought leaves us with the feeling of one step forward, two steps back. Frustrating! Your loved one may appear to undercut his own efforts, diminishing the importance of all the work it took to get to that point. These thoughts are so powerful that they can even undermine the biology of treatment by introducing doubt into every effort. Indeed, each negative thought adds another dose of depression to one's life.

I've developed a mantra to help my patients deal with the morphing of depression. It is as follows: *I need to be conscious of my need to be vigilant about managing my thoughts and words.* That's their homework and part of their ongoing treatment.

What does this mean? I tell my patients that managing these thoughts is like increasing the dosage of their antidepressant medications. In effect, they can diminish the virulence of their depressive thoughts by paying attention to them, watching them morph, catching them, not attaching to them, and observing them without believing them. The better they are at catching and managing these thoughts, the more effective the dosage. This can be a full-time job, but it is one that can help rein in the Four Horsemen!

For instance, Claire drove into a parking spot and waved to the parking attendant. When he didn't respond, she consciously caught the thought that jumped into her mind: "See nobody likes you, not even the parking man!" Since she had been practicing her mantra, she instead found herself laughing at how quickly such a thought could ruin her afternoon.

ELECTROCONVULSIVE THERAPY (ECT)

Many of us have terrible visions of torture chambers when we imagine our loved one receiving electroconvulsive therapy. Fortunately, today these treatments are performed as humanely and as painlessly as possible. They are given after the individual is sedated with a short-acting anesthetic and a muscle relaxant. Patients neither feel nor remember the treatment.

Electroconvulsive therapy seems to work quickly and effectively in cases of severe resistant depression. It may be especially beneficial for an individual who has engaged in a serious suicide attempt or is actively homicidal. ECT is often helpful when a depressed individual becomes psychotic and experiences delusions and hallucinations. Also, individuals who suffer from severe medical illnesses may be unable to participate in psychotherapy or tolerate antidepressant medication but may be able to receive effective treatment with ECT.

Usually, six to twelve treatments are given in intervals of two to three days. They are highly effective and are the fastest way to literally "jolt" an individual out of a severe depression. It is believed that the mild electrical current affects the part of the brain that regulates mood and helps to stimulate the production of precursors to the neurotransmitters that seem in such short supply in depressed individuals.

There can be a brief period of memory loss and confusion following treatment but usually this ameliorates itself within an hour, though some may experience more long-term losses. The psychiatrists John H. Greist and James W. Jefferson, internists and professors of psychiatry at the University of Wisconsin Medical School, write in their book, *Depression and Its Treatment,* "A new technique called brief-pulse ECT uses the minimum amount of electricity needed to produce an effective treatment and substantially reduces memory loss after each treatment and over a course of treatments." They document a case in which ECT seemed quite effective. Their patient, an elderly woman suffering from heart failure and diabetes, was extremely agitated as a result of her depression, which was life-threatening, as it interfered with her care and aggravated her heart condition.

"Though in very poor physical condition," they write, "she tolerated and responded promptly to three electroconvulsive treatments on successive days. Relieved of her depression and constant agitation, she became cooperative with her cardiac and diabetic treatments and progressed to recovery."

MEDICAL HOPE FOR RESISTANT DEPRESSION: THE STAR*D RESEARCH PROJECT

As we've outlined, because resistant depression can be all-pervasive, most often it is treated with psychotherapy coupled with medications. The National Institute of Mental Health (NIMH), the government agency charged with researching the origins and treatments of mental illnesses, has been conducting a federally funded, large-scale, long-term study of the effectiveness of anti-depressants that's called the STAR*D Study. STAR*D stands for Sequenced Treatment Alternatives to Relieve Depression. Although the study is ongoing, results that might be helpful to you were reported in late 2006.

Over a seven-year period, researchers from 41 clinical sites around the country enrolled 2,876 outpatients between the ages of 18 and 75 in the study. These people come from a broad range of ethnic and socioeconomic groups. All of the participants had been diagnosed with major depressive disorder (also called MDD) and had sought treatment for it. MDD is a chronic form of depression, frequently recurring for two or more episodes that can last two years or more—what I have characterized as resistant depression. Patients were referred to the study by their physicians.

Since the goal of the research project was to assess the effec-tiveness of medical treatments for resistant depression, these 2,976 patients were given the antidepressant Celexa for twelve to fourteen weeks. As I explained in Chapter 7, Celexa is a selective serotonin reuptake inhibitor (SSRI). It was chosen because it's not generally associated with troublesome withdrawal symp-toms, it's easy to take (once a day), and it seems to be safe for older adults and patients who are medically fragile. Dosages were carefully controlled based on side effects.

Those whose symptoms were alleviated by this medication moved into a 12-month follow-up program during which they continued on Celexa and were monitored weekly. The criteria for shifting into the follow-up program was not just *some* progress but *remission*—the total absence of symptoms. People who reach this goal generally function better socially and at work, and have a better chance of staying well than do people who only achieve a partial response to their medications.

At level 1, about one-third of the participants reached remission and 10 to 15 percent more responded but did not reach remission. Still, these are considered good results because study participants had high rates of chronic or recurrent depression and other psychiatric medical problems. That means that nearly 50 percent of those with resistant depressions experienced remission or near-remission. But patience is called for. It took an average of six weeks of treatment for participants to improve enough to reach a response and nearly seven weeks for them to achieve remission. Twenty-one percent of the participants withdrew after level 1.

What happened to the rest of the patients? Fourteen hundred and thirty-nine of the participants (about half) either continued to have symptoms or found that Celexa's side effects were intolerable. They moved on to level 2 of the program. Now study participants were given the option of switching to a new medication or adding another one onto their existing dosage of Celexa. Those who switched were randomly prescribed Zoloft, Wellbutrin, or Effexor. These are three different types of medications: Zoloft is an SSRI much like the Celexa; Wellbutrin belongs to another class of antidepressants that work on different neurotransmitters than the SSRIs; and Effexor is a "dual-action" medication that works on two neurotransmitters at the same time.

Those who decided to add on new medications were prescribed either the non-SSRI Wellbutrin, or BuSpar, which is not an antidepressant but enhances the action of antidepressant medications. Participants could also switch to or add cognitive psychotherapy. Thirty percent of the participants withdrew after level 2. This is important to keep in mind as a strengthened ally. There is a tremendous challenge to continue in face of adversity.

The study continued with 377 patients in level 3. It's important to note here how many patients had gone into remission at

Treatment Choices Throughout STAR*D

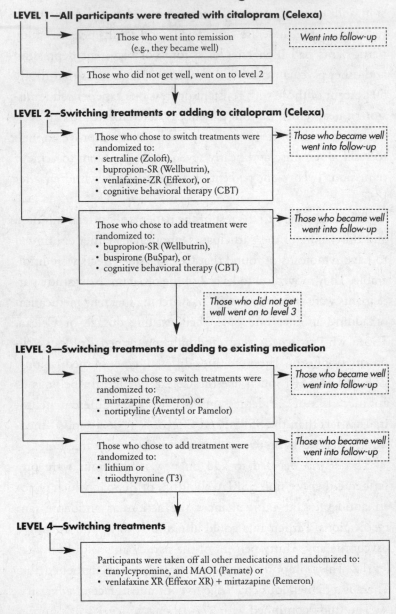

LEVEL 1—All participants were treated with citalopram (Celexa)

Those who went into remission (e.g., they became well)

Went into follow-up

Those who did not get well, went on to level 2

LEVEL 2—Switching treatments or adding to citalopram (Celexa)

Those who chose to switch treatments were randomized to:
- sertraline (Zoloft),
- bupropion-SR (Wellbutrin),
- venlafaxine-ZR (Effexor), or
- cognitive behavioral therapy (CBT)

Those who became well went into follow-up

Those who chose to add treatment were randomized to:
- bupropion-SR (Wellbutrin),
- buspirone (BuSpar), or
- cognitive behavioral therapy (CBT)

Those who became well went into follow-up

Those who did not get well went on to level 3

LEVEL 3—Switching treatments or adding to existing medication

Those who chose to switch treatments were randomized to:
- mirtazapine (Remeron) or
- nortiptyline (Aventyl or Pamelor)

Those who became well went into follow-up

Those who chose to add treatment were randomized to:
- lithium or
- triiodthyronine (T3)

Those who became well went into follow-up

LEVEL 4—Switching treatments

Participants were taken off all other medications and randomized to:
- tranylcypromine, and MAOI (Parnate) or
- venlafaxine XR (Effexor XR) + mirtazapine (Remeron)

this stage! At level 3 patients were again given the option either to try additional medications or to switch to new medications. At this point, 42 percent of the participants withdrew after level 3.

The 142 people who continued at level 4 were considered to have highly treatment-resistant depression. They were taken off all of the previous medications and switched to either the MAOI Parnate or a combination of extended release Effexor XR with Remeron. These treatments were chosen for comparison because previous research had suggested that they may be particularly effective in people who have not received sufficient benefit from other medications.

WHAT CAN WE LEARN FROM THE STAR*D RESULTS?

The nation's largest real-world study of resistant depression, directly comparing treatment strategies, has given us a lot of useful information. First, the good news: SSRIs work for a lot of people. A wide range of effective treatment choices is available, and many people with resistant depression go into remission. According to the NIMH, "studies have shown that most individuals suffering from moderate and severe depression, even those with suicidal thoughts, can substantially benefit from antidepressant medication treatment."

Even if the initial treatment with one SSRI fails, about one in four patients who switch to another medication will get better, regardless of whether the second medication is another SSRI or a different class of drug. And if patients choose to add a new medication to the existing SSRI, about one in three people will get better. Over the course of the four levels in the STAR*D research, about 70 percent of those who didn't withdraw from the study became *symptom-free*. That's good news.

Indeed, according to NIMH publications, "An overall analysis of the STAR*D results indicates that patients with difficult-to-treat depression can get well after trying several treatment strategies." But there is also a proviso: "Those who become symptom-free have a better chance of remaining well than those who experience only symptom *improvement*." You and your loved one must bear in mind that the odds of beating depression diminish with every additional treatment strategy needed. And researchers also found that those who undergo several treatment steps before they become symptom-free are more likely to relapse during the follow-up period. This may be true because patients who required more treatment levels "tended to have more severe depressive symptoms and more coexisting psychiatric and general medical problems at the beginning of the study than those who became well after just one treatment level."

Also, you should note that the more levels a patient had to traverse, the more likely it was that he or she would withdraw from the study. Treating resistant depression can be hard work. This is important information for you as a strengthened ally, and it emphasizes why persistence and perseverance are so important. As in Claire's case, you and your loved one should not give up if the initial medication does not result in a "cure." Continue to work with the doctors to find the best strategy. Your loved one's medical team must pay attention to his individual needs. To avoid relapse, doctors should diligently monitor symptoms and side effects during treatment and even after your loved one becomes symptom-free.

In addition, patience is required. While some people may experience benefits in the first six weeks of treatment, full benefits may not be evident for 10 or 12 weeks. During this time, doctors should work with your loved one to adjust dosages and avoid stopping a treatment prematurely.

Despite all of this useful information, STAR*D still leaves many questions unanswered. We do not yet know the effects of cognitive therapy in place of or in addition to medications—folks enrolled in the STAR*D study were allowed to select their next treatment choice, and many preferred medications to psychotherapy. We have not yet identified why some people experience relapses. We still don't know who will respond to which treatments or whether giving medications in combination at the outset of treatment is more effective than starting with just one and adding or changing as you go.

As a strengthened ally for your loved one with resistant depression, it is clear that treatment is not a start and stop option but a long-term strategy that requires consistent care. The people in this study who were the most severely depressed were also the ones most likely to suffer a relapse within a year. They needed continual monitoring and follow-up.

Sometimes we're limited in our view of what lies ahead. Scientific research is often confusing, especially to the lay person. One day, we read with excitement a newspaper article about an innovative protocol. The next month, these findings are challenged or discredited. We're unsure how to proceed. STAR*D gives us a bigger picture of what is possible in terms of treatments, and these seem to be promising for many people with severe depression. In my years of working with people with cancer and other life-threatening illnesses, I have found that sometimes long-term care is really all about maintenance until the next new treatment comes along. And it could be a new treatment that finally does the trick.

That brings me to exciting new research in the field of mental health.

THE HUMAN GENOME PROJECT AND NEW HOPE FOR CURING DEPRESSION

One aspect of the STAR*D study was the voluntary collection of blood samples from more than 1,900 of the participants. These will allow researchers to identify potential biological markers of the course of the disease, and appropriate treatment responses. They may also help in finding genetic markers for depression, a hot new area for research.

While working on a different book project, my wife, Susan, recently had the rare opportunity to interview Dr. Tom Insel, the director of the National Institute of Mental Health. He spoke with enthusiasm and hope about what lies ahead.

"In 1999," he explained "if you had talked to most people interested in mental illness and brain research, they would tell you about serotonin and maybe dopamine and norepinephrine and receptors for those neurotransmitters. But today we know that there are hundreds, maybe thousands of other players. In fact, we often say that 99 percent of what has been written thus far only covers about 1 percent of the genome. Partly because of the human genome project . . . and partly because the advent of neuro-imaging . . . [science] has allowed us to look inside the brain for the first time. We're just beginning to know who the players are at the genetic level and who the players are at the level of brain circuits. Until the last couple of years we really didn't have a very good idea at all about the circuitry for depression . . . but we're getting that. So this is a very exciting time."

Researchers are now studying groups of genes to determine what sequence may predispose one to depression. They're carefully examining areas in the brain to see whether excessive or insufficient brain activity in certain spots is more likely to predict depressive thoughts. They're asking questions such as whether medications can be designed to be more effective by being tailored to certain genetic patterns. They're wondering how medication and therapy actually work, and they're finding some answers.

"We have a very good picture of what happens when you get better from depression," Dr. Insel continued. "And when you get better with medication it is the same thing as when you get better with psychotherapy. One of the conclusions that people have come up with is that whether it's psychotherapy or Prozac . . . the one thing that seems to consistently happen is that one part of the prefrontal cortex goes from being overactive to becoming less active. And that area—talk about a frontier area—it didn't even have a name before—we call it Area-25. . . . Even though psychotherapy and medication get you there in a different way through a different set of circuits, they both overlap at that point."

It's clear from Dr. Insel's interview that research into the causes and cures for resistant depression is moving quite rapidly. It is therefore important to stay informed. In the Appendix, you'll find some Web sites that are reliable sources of information. They are updated continually, so you can stay on top of the latest developments.

I know that strengthened allies try everything. Your effort matters.

And you may be heartened to know that although Claire still suffers from depression, she has acquired some of the tools to help her manage her negative thoughts and destructive impulses. She has completed her first year of college and is continuing to find new challenges like living in a college dorm and staying focused. It is the feeling that no matter what, we will get through this together that is encouraging for Claire, her parents, and me.

Understanding the incredible range of treatment options available for your depressed loved one is essential to you in your role as strengthened ally, as is your faith in his ability to recover. Healing is possible. As William Styron writes of his recuperation, "Although I was still shaky I knew I had emerged into the light. I felt myself no longer a husk but a body with some of the body's sweet juices stirring again. I had my first dream in many months, confused but to this day imperishable, with a flute in it somewhere, and a wild goose, and a dancing girl."

CHAPTER 9

Depression and Chronic Illness

LAURIE, AN ACCOUNTANT IN HER FIFTIES, BECAME depressed several months after a diagnosis of breast cancer. Not only was she despondent that she had the disease, but the chemotherapy treatments exhausted her and exacerbated her pessimistic moods. Together, these factors made her less willing to continue treatment. "What's the use?" she moaned to her husband. "I'm going to die anyway."

Laurie's case is not unusual. People with serious or life-threatening illnesses are at greater risk for depression than those who are not ill. Indeed, depression does not often occur in a vacuum but is accompanied by a wide variety of chronic and infectious diseases. The World Health Organization recently estimated that although 10 percent of the world's population suffers from depression, nearly 35 percent of cancer patients are depressed. The depression numbers are higher for people suffering from other illnesses as well. About 23 percent of heart attack patients, 28 percent of those with high blood pressure, 27 percent of diabetes patients, and nearly 45 percent of people with HIV/AIDS also have depression.

This co-occurrence of depression with another illness is called co-morbidity, and it is the subject of a good deal of research these days. According to Thom Bornemann, director of the Mental Health Program at the Carter Center in Atlanta, Georgia, "Co-morbid depression . . . is neither a chance phenomenon nor a mere feeling of demoralization or sadness brought on by the hardships of chronic illness. While the prevalence of major depression in the general population can go from an average of 3 percent up to 10 percent, it is consistently higher in people affected by chronic disease."

"WOULDN'T YOU FEEL DEPRESSED IF YOU HAD CANCER?"

This is a question I've often heard from cancer patients, their families, and friends. It's also a question that might be posed by nursing staff and physicians. But according to Dr. Andrew Roth, a psychiatrist at Memorial Sloan Kettering Cancer Center in Manhattan, "It may seem logical to expect that someone facing any life-threatening illness would experience some sadness or depression. However, the problem of depression in medically ill patients is a more complex issue. It can span from normal reactions to bad news to clinically

significant disorders that can benefit from a variety of treatments."
Depression is a separate illness that should be diagnosed and
treated even if your loved one is undergoing treatment for a chronic
or life-threatening illness. This is true not only for cancer and the illnesses listed above. Symptoms of conditions such as Parkinson's
disease, hypoglycemia, chronic fatigue syndrome, renal failure, and
others may include feelings of depression.

As clinical social worker Irene Pollin indicates in her book,
Taking Charge: Overcoming the Challenges of Long-Term Illness,
research suggests that individuals with long-term illnesses have a
greater incidence of emotional distress than those who are well.
She writes, "If you are ill, you may become fearful and depressed
or enraged. You may withdraw from friends and family—the support network you so sorely need at this vulnerable time—out of
fear of dependency, abandonment, or stigmatization. You may
even perceive your health as being worse than it actually is."

Although it is to be expected that your loved one will feel
upset, anxious, and stressed when facing one of these illnesses, if
these feelings and the sense of hopelessness become pervasive
and interfere with normal functioning, they must be recognized
and treated. It can be dangerous for your loved one when depression accompanies life-threatening illnesses, especially because ill-
ness-associated depression impairs your loved one's quality of
life and also his or her motivation to strive for recovery.

WHICH CAME FIRST: DEPRESSION OR CANCER?

So you might ask, did the depression contribute to the illness or
did the illness bring on the depression? This is a classic chicken-
and-egg conundrum that leads to a classic paradoxical answer—
it's both. The two are quite intertwined.

One way to understand this conundrum is by using cancer as an example. Research shows that cancer and depression often occur together. This could be biological: The tumors themselves can cause hormonal and chemical changes in the body that trigger the disturbed sleep patterns, fatigue, malaise, pain, and low energy that are similar to the physiological symptoms of depression. And, as you may know, cancer treatments such as chemotherapy, radiation, and surgery can also lead to extreme fatigue, sleeplessness, loss of appetite, and pain. These are predictable, or *reliable,* responses to the illness and its treatments.

It's clear that many of these biological factors, coupled with the side effects of cancer treatment, overlap with symptoms of depression. But there are emotional issues to consider as well. For instance, your loved one can experience the disease as a traumatic event with multiple stressors—the diagnostic tests and the anxiety they provoke, the moment the doctor pronounces the dreaded diagnosis, the pain involved in surgical treatment and hospitalization, the discomforts of radiation and chemotherapy, the side effects of treatment, and the fear of recurrence are all emotionally traumatic aspects of the illness.

In fact, distress is the most underreported symptom associated with the diagnosis and treatment of cancer. Even though the World Health Organization's estimates are lower, other research shows that nearly 47 percent of cancer patients are suffering from distress that would be classified as a depressive or anxiety disorder as defined by the *DSM-IV-TR,* the psychiatric diagnostic manual. No wonder there is a challenge in figuring out whether these symptoms are solely linked to the illness or actually triggered by depression.

Unfortunately, no matter what the cause, depression is often underdiagnosed and untreated in cancer patients because people, including many health-care workers, believe that depression is a "normal" or reasonable reaction to a devastating illness. In fact, studies have shown that oncologists and oncology nurses do not easily recognize even severe depression in their patients. Family members and medical personnel may attribute the loss of appetite, sleep disturbances, low energy, fatigue, and other disturbing symptoms to the cancer and its treatments, but these may mimic or mask underlying emotional distress. Failing to consider that depression may be causing some of these symptoms may cause your loved one's mental health to be overlooked even while he's getting the very best oncological care.

And that leads to the other part of the conundrum. Although research has made clear that we don't "give ourselves" cancer, studies show that a depressed patient is less likely to adhere to recommended treatments and screening procedures than one who isn't depressed. Although depression does not cause cancer, its affects can certainly contribute to the cancer's progression as well as to despair and hopelessness. All of these factors add to the misery of cancer and to much poorer quality of life for your loved one and the whole family.

DEPRESSION AND DIABETES

Diabetes coupled with depression is also a "tough combination," according to William Polonsky, Ph.D., at the University of California, San Diego. As he explains in his book, *Diabetes Burnout: What to Do When You Can't Take It Anymore,* "Depression can make it more difficult to manage diabetes, and in turn, diabetes can make it harder to recognize and treat depression." And again, it is not unusual for depression to accompany diabetes—it is three times more common in diabetics than in those who do not have the condition. Middle-aged women are particularly at risk.

These statistics are all the more worrisome because the depression that accompanies diabetes can be especially stubborn. In some studies, 80 percent of diabetics with major depression who were treated with antidepressants had relapses within a five-year period. The average person in these studies suffered four 14-month-long episodes.

Much like cancer, diabetes increases the likelihood that your loved one will become depressed, and this is especially true if the illness is not controlled. High blood glucose levels can make your loved one feel depleted and sluggish. They actually affect her mood, pushing her toward gloominess and exhaustion. This may happen so gradually that no one realizes that a change has occurred until the problem has become severe. Significant fluctuations in blood glucose levels (big highs and lows) are also exhausting and can open the door to depression.

As with cancer, diabetes and depression can also intertwine with each other, worsening the progression of both illnesses. The lethargy and lack of motivation that accompanies depression can undermine your loved one's willingness to watch her diet and test her blood sugar regularly. This can cause sugar levels to spike, worsening the depression and giving rise to more lethargy, inaction, and despair. In the end, a dangerous cycle takes over.

How can you and your loved one deal with these issues? First, it's paramount that she seek out a thorough medical evaluation to determine what's causing the symptoms. As with all other medical conditions coupled with depression, there may be other physiological factors at work here. For instance, a malfunctioning thyroid gland can also produce depressive symptoms. Some prescription medications may be at fault. Once the source of the depression is identified, you should work together to develop a treatment plan that includes psychotherapy and likely medications (see Chapters 6–8).

However, Dr. Polonsky strongly recommends that depressed diabetes patients refrain from attempts at self-medication, especially with alcohol. Alcohol or recreational drugs may provide a temporary sense of escape, but like all cases of depression, they cause worsening moods over time because they prevent your loved one from getting restful sleep. Alcohol also raises blood sugar levels. "If you are suffering with depression and you are drinking excessively," he writes, "you are pouring gasoline onto a fire. At this stage seeking outside help is critical."

It's also clear that your loved one should pay special attention to managing her blood sugar levels. Tighter control of blood glucose can, in some cases, help resolve the depression. And a sunnier mood can provide the impetus for continued careful sugar monitoring and follow-up, creating a positive and more healthful cycle.

DEPRESSION AND HEART DISEASE

According to the National Institute of Mental Health, two decades of research have shown that people with depression are at greater risk of developing heart disease than people who are not depressed. And, conversely, people with heart disease are at greater risk for developing depression than those who are healthy. Although 10 percent of the American public may suffer from depression, the numbers increase tremendously for those who have heart disease—all the way to 33 percent. Even more alarmingly, people with heart disease who are also depressed have an increased risk of death after a heart attack compared to those who are not depressed. The bottom line is: "The combination of depression and heart disease is associated with increased sickness and death."

Depression and anxiety contribute to heart disease by affecting your loved one's heart rhythms, increasing blood pressure, and altering blood clotting. Depression and anxiety can also raise cholesterol and insulin levels. They can give rise to chronically high levels of the stress hormones adrenaline and cortisol. "As high levels of stress hormones signal a 'fight or flight' reaction," NIMH experts explain, "the body's metabolism is diverted away from the type of tissue repair needed in heart disease."

Unfortunately, as with other illnesses, depression may make it harder for your loved one to follow treatment recommendations. And heart disease patients who are also depressed seem to take longer to recover. According to Sylvia G. Simpson, a professor at the Johns Hopkins Medical Institutions in Baltimore, these individuals are the least likely to have returned to work or to have reduced their risk factors (such as smoking) six months after their heart attacks. As with other illnesses, even the medical doctor may overlook or misinterpret the symptoms of depression, mistaking them for symptoms of heart disease or the result of a heart attack. It is, therefore, extremely important that your loved one receive a correct diagnosis for depression. Also be aware that some antidepressants can interact with heart medications so it is vital that your loved one communicate with the psychiatrist about all of the medications he is taking. However, proper treatment for depression will help your loved one better manage both diseases, enhancing his survival as well as his quality of life.

DEPRESSION AND PARKINSON'S DISEASE

According to a publication of the National Parkinson Foundation, major depression is present in approximately 20 to 40 percent of Parkinson's disease patients at any given time, but the lifetime incidence of depression for these patients is estimated at from 40 to 90 percent. Indeed, Parkinson's patients have higher rates of depression than patients with other chronic illnesses who have the same level of disability. Depression may even precede the onset of the disease.

Anxiety, apathy, low energy, the inability to feel pleasure, and decreased sex drive are often diagnosed in people with Parkinson's disease. Why should this be so? Again, part of the problem relates to the biology of the illness and not just its debilitating symptoms of tremor, rigidity, and slowness of movement. Research suggests that depression in Parkinson's results from disease-related degenerative changes in the brain that deplete levels of the neurotransmitters dopamine, noradrenaline, and serotonin. Damage to dopamine pathways in the brain as well as areas that play a role in pleasure and reward-seeking behavior can lead to depressed moods and apathy.

As with the other serious illnesses I've covered above, the depression is often difficult to diagnose in Parkinson's disease patients because of the overlap of the condition's symptoms with depression. Parkinson expert Dr. Abraham Lieberman explains that "people with Parkinson disease who move slowly, have an expressionless face, and speak softly may appear depressed when they're not, while depressed people who move slowly, have an expressionless face, and speak softly may appear to have Parkinson disease when they don't." A careful analysis of symptoms is paramount for your loved one, especially because apathy, anxiety, lack of energy, the inability to feel pleasure, and loss of libido—all potential Parkinson symptoms—are more frequent and debilitating when they occur with depression.

DEPRESSION AND STROKE

Although strokes (caused by bleeding or a blood clot in the brain) can occur in all age groups, according to the National

Institute of Mental Health they are most prevalent in people over the age of 65. Indeed, about three-quarters of all strokes occur in people of that age group, making it a leading cause of disability among the elderly. Of the 600,000 people who suffer a stroke each year, an estimated 10 to 27 percent also experience major depression. An additional 15 to 40 percent experience at least some symptoms of depression within two months of the attack.

On average, untreated depression in a person who has suffered a stroke lasts for just under a year. The factors that influence the likelihood of your loved one developing depression, as well as the duration of the depression, include: the location of the brain lesion, a previous bout with depression, a family history of depression, and his social functioning before the stroke.

Although a stroke is a brain disease, it can affect your loved one's entire body. Paralysis, cognitive deficits, speech impairment, emotional difficulties, fatigue, and trouble with daily living skills are a few of the disabilities that may result. Many people require psychological or psychiatric help after a stroke. Depression, anxiety, frustration, and anger are common.

Despite the enormous advances in brain research in the last twenty years, depression is often undiagnosed (and therefore untreated) in people who have suffered a stroke. You, your loved one, and even your medical team may misinterpret symptoms of depression as an inevitable reaction to the effects of the stroke. But depression is a separate illness that should be diagnosed and treated. Stroke survivors who are also depressed (and particularly those suffering from major depression) may be less willing to participate in rehabilitation exercises and may be more irritable. They may even experience personality changes. On the other hand, treatment for the depression can shorten the rehab process, lead to a more rapid recovery, and even allow your loved one to return to his normal routine more quickly. An extra benefit is a savings in health-care costs, especially if nursing home expenses can be eliminated.

But it's especially important that your loved one's treatment for depression after a stroke be managed by someone in the mental health field—a psychiatrist, psychologist, or clinical social worker—who is in close contact with the physician providing the post-stroke rehab and treatment. The involvement of a psychiatrist is especially critical if antidepressants are prescribed, in order to avoid harmful drug interactions. No matter how severe the stroke, however, your loved one does not have to suffer from depression. Effective treatments are available.

DEPRESSION AND HIV/AIDS

HIV/AIDS is often accompanied by depression—as many as one in three HIV patients suffers from it. You and your loved one (as well as his medical team) may make the faulty assumption that depression is an inevitable reaction to being diagnosed with AIDS, especially since it can be a terribly incapacitating illness. Many people are so debilitated they are unable to hold a steady job or take care of their own households. Others may experience phases of intense life-threatening illness followed by relative calm.

Some of the symptoms of depression can be due to HIV, specific HIV-related disorders, or medication side effects. A depressive syndrome is a separate illness that should be treated even if your loved one is undergoing treatment for HIV or AIDS. A skilled health professional will recognize the symptoms of depression and will do a proper assessment. He or she will also suggest an appropriate treatment plan that can include antidepressants and psychotherapy.

Again, it's important to take action as soon as possible. According to the National Institute of Mental Health, episodes of depression may be triggered by stress, difficult life events, or the effects of HIV on the brain: "Whatever its origin, depression can limit the energy needed to keep focused on staying healthy, and research shows that it may accelerate HIV's progression to AIDS." Obviously, it should be treated.

People with HIV generally tolerate prescription antidepressant medications well; however, drug interactions can occur and side effects may need careful monitoring. Some people try to treat their depression with herbal remedies, but the use of these supplements should be discussed with a physician before any regimen is begun. For instance, St. John's Wort has been promoted to treat mild depression, but recent research shows it can have harmful interactions with other medications, including those prescribed for HIV. This allows the AIDS virus to rebound, perhaps in a drug-resistant form.

Finally, if your loved one has HIV/AIDS, he will need more than access to good medical care to stay healthy. According to the NIMH, "Determination and discipline are also required to deal with the stresses of avoiding high-risk behaviors, keeping up with the latest scientific advances, adhering to complicated medication regimens, reshuffling schedules for doctor visits, and grieving over the death of loved ones." These important and complicated tasks are made all the more difficult if your loved one is depressed. And he doesn't have to be. Treatments are available.

TREATING DEPRESSION WHEN YOUR LOVED ONE IS SERIOUSLY ILL

Because of the many medical conditions that can cause feelings of depression, it's imperative for your loved one to have a thorough physical when symptoms of depression first become evident. An accurate diagnosis will rule out any medical conditions and must precede treatment for depression.

It's also important for your loved one's physician to consider whether an illness itself, if present, or the medications being used to treat the medical condition can be causing depression. For instance, imbalances in the hormones secreted by the endocrine glands (such as the thyroid, parathyroid, and adrenal glands) can also cause symptoms of depression. In these cases, if one corrects the hormone imbalance—by giving synthetic thyroxine, the hormone the thyroid normally secretes, to an individual who is not producing enough—the symptoms generally disappear. And as you've seen from my discussion of diabetes, sometimes controlling the blood glucose levels more tightly has the equally positive effect of reining in the depression too.

According to Andrew Roth, "Sometimes just the knowledge of the cause of feeling differently is enough to help the patient cope better. If a change in treatment of the medical illness that will not change the outcome can be made, your loved one may tolerate it better with less depression. And sometimes an antidepressant may be useful."

Physicians and psychiatrists must also find out if there are any known interactions between the proposed antidepressant treatment and any medications your loved one is already taking. "Starting low in dosage and going up slowly" is sometimes a useful guideline, Dr. Roth adds. The choice of antidepressants may also depend on your loved one's condition. For instance, if she is experiencing fatigue related to her illness, an antidepressant that may have some energizing effects can be helpful. Similarly, if she has anxiety or insomnia, an antidepressant that is more calming may be beneficial. If your loved one has been having some gastric upset due to her illness or medications, an antidepressant such as Remeron may be considered. In these instances, it's clear that you will all benefit from working with a medical professional who is well versed not only in the medical condition your loved one is coping with but also in mood enhancing medications.

Whatever you and your loved one decide to do, it's important to remember that depression is a treatable disorder. It can and should be addressed in addition to whatever medical condition you are all facing. There is no need for your loved one to suffer from depression in addition to another serious medical illness, since allowing depression to persist undermines recovery and increases the misery quotient for all of you. That's just like rubbing salt in a wound.

◆

CHAPTER 10

Creative
Alternatives

Overcoming the blues and depression can take many forms. Any activity that gives you and your loved one pleasure can augment the more formal approaches described in Chapters 6 through 8. There are many activities and some lifestyle adjustments you might not have considered that may help immeasurably. Let's look at some of these now.

FOUR SIMPLE WAYS TO
BEAT THE BLUES

The bluse are easier to dispel than a serious depression; in fact, they are very amenable to distractions! So if your loved one has the blues you might prevent her ruminations from turning into a full-fledged depressive episode by trying the following ideas:

1. Seek out diverting entertainment. Take your loved one to see a new blockbuster movie, particularly a comedy or action-adventure. Offer her a great mystery novel by a favorite author. Attend an exciting sporting event together. Escapist fare has its purpose.

2. Enjoy sensual treats and pleasures. For some, trying a highly touted restaurant or shopping for a new outfit are excellent diversions from negative thoughts. Eating favorite foods or treating your loved one to a surprise romantic candlelit dinner can also eradicate the blues. Try dual massages, a trip to the spa for pampering, or even a yoga retreat.

3. Pull weeds. Sometimes, experiencing a sense of closure or success can chase away the blues. My wife often calms herself by pulling weeds. Others find that painting the patio furniture, waxing the car, or baking a pie are small chores that can give one a big sense of completion and control.

4. Volunteer. Helping others in need is a mighty distractor. It reminds your loved one that others may be in worse shape than she is and can divert her from ruminating on her own life. Volunteering to coach children's sports teams can be uplifting and enjoyable. Besides, it can provide a great opportunity for exercising, and that's one of the key alternative approaches for dealing with a full-blown depression.

EXERCISE

Exercise is easy. It's free. It's fun. It's health enhancing. There are no side effects. It can help prevent future depressive episodes. And you and your loved one can do it together.

So what's the downside? There isn't one!

Numerous research studies have documented how aerobic exercise (dancing, playing basketball, jogging, biking, swimming, hiking, and so on) and nonaerobic exercise (such as weight training) can alleviate mild to moderate depression and enhance the effectiveness of treatments for more severe depression. Even a low-intensity activity like walking works. Simply engaging in a regular regimen may be a powerful tonic for the blues. It could be all that your loved one needs.

Exercise is so effective that when it is used in combination with psychotherapy and/or medication your loved one's response will be better than if she depended on these treatment protocols alone.

The effects of exercise can be long-term. One study of five thousand college students enrolled in a mental health course found that those who participated in regular exercise and continued to do so for seven years after leaving the course experienced decreased depression and anxiety. Exercise, when taken together with other approaches, can become a potent weapon in your loved one's fight against depression.

Why is exercise so effective? There are several theories to explain it. On a psychological level, it may be that the activity distracts your loved one from her feelings of pain and loss. Or, in winning a round of golf or jogging around the block, she may gain a sense of mastery that can combat her feelings of hopelessness and despair. Exercise, especially if it's in the context of team sports, dancing, or aerobics classes, can also allay some of her sense of isolation.

Moreover, activities that take us out into nature such as hiking and skiing or simply walking in the woods can be good for the soul. A *Wall Street Journal* writer, Timothy Aeppel, reported that one woman in treatment with an ecotherapist, a new breed of psychotherapists who specialize in the ecological aspects of mental states, overcame her depression by taking daily five-mile walks through New York's Central Park. "I feel better than I have in years," she is reported to have said.

The positive effects of movement can also derive from biological sources. Scientists have found that physical activity releases chemicals in the brain called endorphins. These have a morphine-like effect: They reduce the experience of pain and create feelings of elation. Activity also seems to improve the action and metabolism of neurotransmitters such as norepinephrine and serotonin. Deep breathing increases oxygen flow and helps to reduce anxiety. These are essential for the regulation of mood.

How much exercise is enough? According to Dr. George Nicoloff at St. Mary's Hospital in Grand Rapids, Michigan, and Thomas L. Schwenk, a sports medicine expert who teaches at the University of Michigan Medical School, a program of aerobic exercise two to five times per week for thirty to forty minutes with five to ten minutes of both warm-up and cool-down should suffice. The activity should be challenging without being so difficult as to engender a sense of failure or inferiority—that would be self-defeating! It should also be varied and fun.

Drs. Nicoloff and Schwenk remind us that "the threshold of self-defeat for depressed patients is probably lower than for non-depressed persons." No exercise regimen will work if your loved one finds it too difficult to be successful. She should begin with easier activities and increase the intensity as she masters them.

Failures can cause emotional setbacks and exacerbate your loved one's feelings of inadequacy and loss, so she should be realistic about her goals. A friendly, noncompetitive game of tennis in which you cooperate at keeping a rally going may be more beneficial than playing to win. Your loved one will be more likely to come back for more if she has had fun.

Of course, no exercise routine will work if your loved one is unwilling to participate in it. A depressed person may have a hard time getting up for any activity. Going for a short walk together, just to get some air, is a start. Something is better than nothing.

Focus on the small steps toward the goal. Also, your loved one may be more motivated to work out if the activity is convenient and does not disrupt the rest of her daily schedule.

There is just one small risk with exercise. A few individuals become addicted to the altered mood states that exercise creates. Signs of addiction include needing an ever-increasing "dose" of exercise in order to achieve the positive effects; the relegation to secondary status of work and/or family relationships for the sake of a training regimen; and a tendency to elevate "feeling good" to being more important than anything else. There can be too much of a good thing. Sometimes, overinvolvement in exercise can be an indication of obsessive-compulsive disorder. Should these circumstances arise, they should be incorporated into therapeutic discussion and treatment. Aristotle recommended many years ago, "Moderation in all things." That includes the use of exercise to combat depression.

FOOD

We all know that food can affect our general health—our cholesterol levels, our bone density, even our risks for getting certain cancers. More and more, scientists are also linking what we eat with how we feel emotionally.

Judith J. Wurtman, a researcher at the Massachusetts Institute of Technology, reports that people use food, especially carbohydrates, to make themselves feel better when they are in negative emotional states. They experience a temporary improvement in their mood following a carbohydrate-rich meal or snack.

Reading Dr. Wurtman's research brought back to mind images of my mother wandering the house late at night, eating Rocky Road ice cream straight from the half-gallon container. It was one of her methods to temporarily make herself feel better, and her weight would fluctuate according to her emotional state. It seems funny now to think of her "self-medicating" with ice cream. If only that solution had been permanent!

How do carbohydrates alter mood? Dr. Wurtman theorizes that they release insulin, which suppresses most large amino acids from entering the brain with the exception of tryptophan, a precursor of serotonin. With relatively higher levels of tryptophan entering the brain, more serotonin is manufactured and can circulate. Higher serotonin levels are thought to be associated with improved moods.

The effect of carbohydrate-rich food can be much like that of the antidepressant medications, except the medications are much stronger and they stay in the body longer. And of course sugar is a temporary fix.

Some people use carbohydrate-rich foods (including chocolate) as a form of self-medication. Unfortunately, this can put them in the fast lane to obesity. Dr. Wurtman reports on research studies in which obese women who craved carbohydrates had lower blood serotonin levels than obese and lean individuals who did not crave these high-sugar foods. She suggests the use of antidepressants such as Prozac, which mimic the effects of carbohydrates, for individuals who overmedicate themselves with food.

In her book, *Mood and Food*, the registered dietician Elizabeth Somer also explores how the foods we eat can heighten depression. "Certain eating habits," she writes, "such as skipping meals may aggravate or even generate negative moods." She also theorizes that the levels and activities of the all-important neurotransmitters are sensitive to what we eat.

The neurotransmitters norepinephrine and dopamine are manufactured by the body from tyrosine, an amino acid found in high-protein foods such as poultry or dairy products, wheat germ, egg yolks, and foods containing the B vitamins, vitamin C, folic acid, iron, and magnesium.

According to Somer, there is a seesaw relationship between tryptophan and tyrosine. "For tryptophan-serotonin levels to rise," she writes, "tyrosine levels must be low; conversely, when tyrosine and its neurotransmitters are in full swing, tryptophan levels are moderate to low." This usually affects our appetites. When we eat a high-carbohydrate meal, like pancakes for breakfast, the increased serotonin levels diminish our desire for starches. The next meal, we're more apt to focus on high-protein, low-carbohydrate foods, such as a turkey sandwich for lunch.

If your loved one's depression is based on low norepineph-rine levels, she may experience some benefit from eating low-carbohydrate, high-protein foods. If that doesn't work, her prob-lem might be due to low serotonin levels. In that case, she might try a diet that includes at least one complex carbohydrate per meal—a bagel, a potato, whole-grain pasta, brown rice, fruit, and so on—along with lean meats and low-fat dairy products.

Somer advises, "Plan a carbohydrate-rich snack, such as whole-grain breads and cereals or a starchy vegetable like a potato or a sweet potato, for that time of the day when you are the most vul-nerable. . . . Do not avoid cravings. . . . You are denying your body the very nutrients it needs to regulate the nerve chemicals and hor-mones that affect mood. . . . Respond to those cravings, but do so in moderation and with planned, nutritious foods."

Some foods should be avoided. Too much caffeine can give your loved one a quick apparent burst of energy but can also lead to fatigue and mood problems. Somer advises taking no more than two servings per day.

She makes some other food recommendations that your loved one may find helpful in combating depression:

- Breakfasts should include one serving each of grains, fruit, and low-fat dairy products. This boosts energy and im-proves mood.

- Rather than three large meals, your loved one might benefit from five to six small meals and snacks spread out over the day. According to Somer, people who spread out their daily intake "are less prone to fatigue, insomnia, and depression and are better able to maintain desirable weight."

- Fat should be limited to no more than 25 percent of the calories consumed daily. (This is advisable for all of us!) Your loved one should eat no more than one serving of sweet or creamy foods per day.

- Your loved one should increase the percentage of complex carbohydrates, fiber, vitamins, and minerals in her diet by eating more vegetables, fruits, and grains. Depression has been linked to vitamin B6 deficiencies. Bananas, avocados, skinless chicken, salmon, potatoes (including skin), dark leafy greens, and oatmeal are rich in this vitamin.

- Many people experience fatigue from low-grade dehydration. Somer suggests drinking at least six 8-ounce glasses of water daily.

- If your depressed loved one has lost her appetite and eats less than 2,500 calories per day, she might benefit from a well-balanced vitamin and mineral supplement that provides 100 to 300 percent of the minimum daily requirements.

The entire family might consider making these positive lifestyle adjustments. You are all partners in the change.

Margie and Joe decided that they would both alter their diets in order to help each other while they worked at overcoming her depression. They reviewed the food suggestions I made and decided on which foods they were willing to give up and which they would eat more of. Together they planned menus, shopped for ingredients, and prepared the meals. They bought cookbooks on low-fat cuisine and tried new recipes. They actually enjoyed making the change in their lifestyle, and Joe lost some extra weight to boot.

SLEEP PATTERNS

Disruptions in sleep patterns—the inability to fall asleep and stay asleep or, conversely, to get out of bed—are often the hallmarks of depression. My mom would often "walk the nights, and sleep the days," as she would say. This worried and saddened her.

According to Dr. Mark S. Gold, a professor at the University of Florida Medical School, research has shown that depressed individuals have mistimed sleep cycles. Their sleeping/waking patterns seem to run "backward." The normal pattern involves several ninety-minute cycles throughout the night, each consisting of four sleep stages plus REM (rapid eye movement) sleep, an almost waking state in which dreaming occurs. For most of us, deep sleep occurs early in the night and REM sleep occupies only a small fraction of the first ninety-minute cycle. As the night progresses, the deep-sleep stages get successively shorter within each cycle, while REM sleep becomes more prominent.

The pattern runs in the opposite direction for depressed individuals. They experience long stretches of REM sleep early in the night. This recedes toward morning. According to Mark Gold, the effect of this reversal is that "depressed people also get less overall deep sleep, which is the most restorative and refreshing of all." Perhaps this is why your depressed loved one may spend long hours sleeping but still awaken feeling exhausted and spent.

This sleep disruption is a sign that your loved one's biological clock, her inner timing mechanism, or circadian rhythm, may be out of kilter. Antidepressant medications return the patterns to their normal order, but Dr. Gold also recommends an easier method: Simply have your loved one stay up for twenty-four hours! This seems to reset the biological clock in depressed individuals—it's "one of the best ways we know to snap somebody out of depression," Dr. Gold writes. The effects may not be long-lasting, but they work for a day or two.

Other strategies that may regulate a malfunctioning biological clock associated with depression include

- taking a carefully monitored dose of the natural sleep hormone melatonin
- shifting the timing of bedtime to five or six hours earlier than normal, then slowly moving it forward to the usual time
- following a strict bedtime/waking and food schedule daily
- avoiding caffeine, drugs (such as No-Doz or Nytol and other stimulants or depressants), and alcohol, which desynchronize one's system
- incorporating a relaxation or breathing exercise similar to the one found in Chapter 4 if there is middle-of-the-night or early-morning awakening.

LIGHT THERAPY

Seasonal affective disorder (SAD) is related to the lengthening and shortening of days as the seasons progress. Individuals afflicted with SAD grow morose as the year wanes. As if getting ready to hibernate for the winter, they have intense food cravings, especially carbohydrates, and experience lethargy, oversleeping, weight gain, and general fatigue during the fall and winter months. (By contrast, those whose depression doesn't seem to cycle with the seasons may experience the opposite symptoms—insomnia, loss of appetite, and agitation—which occur all year round.)

In an interview in Kathy Cronkite's book *On the Edge of Darkness*, Dr. Norman E. Rosenthal, the director of light therapy studies at the National Institute of Mental Health and one of the first to identify SAD as a syndrome, explains that light and latitude have much to do with this type of depression: "Somebody . . . in Maryland who might have had bad seasonal affective disorder might have been disabled when she went up to Toronto and might have felt much better the few years that she lived in Florida and might have been completely cured in Guam."

Scientists now believe that the incidence of SAD is related to how much light hits the retina of the eye. The less light, the more melatonin, a natural sleep hormone, circulates in the body. In scientific experiments, lab animals that were injected with melatonin overate, overslept, and became lethargic. Melatonin is a by-product of serotonin. The more melatonin in the system, the less serotonin. It is possible that an overabundance of melatonin and a concommitent drop in serotonin levels causes this type of depression.

If your loved one is coping with SAD, one of the easiest things she can do is slow the production of melatonin by getting more light during the drearier months. According to Dr. Rosenthal that may mean

- RELOCATING: moving into a home that has big windows and a south or east exposure
- LANDSCAPING: cutting back trees, hedges, and shrubs from the windows to admit more natural light
- REDECORATING: painting walls white and recarpeting with light-colored floor coverings (avoid dark paneling); adding light fixtures and more intense lighting such as halogen lamps to the home

Light therapy (also called phototherapy) is also an option. This involves sitting under lights that are five to ten times brighter than usual for one to two hours each day. Studies have shown that up to 80 percent of people with SAD who undergo this type of therapy report improvement in only four days. If there is no improvement, the light therapy may be carried out more frequently or for longer sessions. Because symptoms do return when one stops this regimen, it is recommended to continue it for the duration of the darker months.

The Wall Street Journal has reported on manufacturers such as Circadian Travel Technologies, in Bethesda, Maryland, which has developed a type of lighted visor that projects more light into the eyes of those who travel a lot to help them cope with jet lag. This new device may be useful for people with SAD. Your loved one's health-care professional may be able to advise her about such a device.

Changing latitudes can also be an option—though an expensive one. One of my retired New York friends who believes he is suffering from SAD spends as much time in Miami and Boca Raton during the winter as he can afford. Even if you can't take months off, planning a winter vacation around a resort close to the Equator rather than a ski trip to Vermont or the Rockies may also allay some of SAD'S effects.

The nutritionist Elizabeth Somer also recommends that someone with SAD avoid caffeine: "SAD sufferers consume more coffee, tea, and colas during the winter months than in other seasons, probably in an attempt to elevate mood and increase energy. However, caffeine's effects on the nervous system . . . can aggravate SAD symptoms."

TWELVE-STEP PROGRAMS

If your loved one's depression is interrelated with drug addiction or alcohol abuse, a 12-step program such a Alcoholics Anonymous might provide valuable support. These structured programs work for many individuals as an adjunct to psychotherapy. The steps toward recovery are concrete, specific, and action-oriented.

Twelve-step programs help combat isolation. Sometimes participants create relationships with "sponsors"—individuals to confide in who are available, experienced in dealing with recovery, and nonjudgmental.

Allied groups for family members such as Al-Anon can be helpful to you as a caregiver. These groups help to clarify enabling and codependency issues and also provide support in times of need.

LITTLE THINGS

There are many other small things that you can do to help your loved one regain a more positive attitude. Here's a sampling:

- Pray together. Religious observance can be a source of hope and spiritual renewal.
- Encourage your loved one to become involved in volunteer activities with the needy. As I mentioned at the opening of this chapter, this may be more realistic for someone with the blues who can gain a perspective on her life's problems when she has the opportunity to get out of herself for a short time.
- Leave self-help books and tapes around the house. Make them available without badgering your loved one about them.

- Bring home videos of comedies. Old sitcoms like *I Love Lucy* broadcast on cable are also enjoyable. Without announcing what you're going to do or asking your loved one's permission, simply start watching. Perhaps she will join you, and laugh with you.
- Listen to music, sing songs, go to concerts. Music can have a healing quality, especially if both of you are feeling depleted.
- Play favorite board games together like chess, Scrabble, or Monopoly. These are distracting and diverting.

In one of her programs, the radio psychologist Toni Grant reported that "thirty seconds of French kissing" had been found to be an effective, immediate treatment for enhancing intimacy and decreasing loneliness and depression! If only it were so simple! But a sense of humor, the ability to make light, can be such a soothing balm that you and your loved one will confidently include it among your depression-fighting tools.

CHAPTER 11

What You Should Expect from the Medical Community

ONE OF MY LONG-TERM PATIENTS, SHANNON, CAME into my office one day, eager to talk about a couples counseling session she had had earlier that week. The other therapist had asked her why she had been seeing me on and off for ten years. Especially in this day and age of managed care and "brief psychotherapy," ten years seemed like a really long time. (Of course, the vast majority of individuals won't need therapy for so long, but there are some cases in which psychological or physical abuse and/or losses have been so severe that long-term therapy is required.)

"I said to her without pausing," Shannon declared, " 'If it hadn't been for Mitch, I would have been dead.' "

The finality of Shannon's statement, and the way she delivered it—stated as a fact, without a flutter of emotion—had stopped the other therapist in her tracks, as it did me.

"When I was twenty and I first came to see you," Shannon continued, "you were the only person in my life who believed me and tried to understand me. I know now that without that support, I would have killed myself. You were my last hope. I haven't been the easiest patient, but that therapist's question crystallized the truth, and I am truly grateful for your help."

I was touched by Shannon's words. I tried to speak, but all that came from my lips were a gulp and a sob. I too recalled those early sessions so many years ago, when week after week, this young woman spent most of the session crying. She would share briefly something of her life in hushed, short sentences. And I was reminded again of the depth of human suffering.

Shannon's depiction of the support she found and her recovery from depression reminded me of an ancient Zen tale about three teachers. It's a parable that illuminates the nurturing and supportive role of the therapist, or anyone directly involved in the helping professions.

The first teacher viewed his pupils as if they were empty vessels into which he would pour information. The second saw his charges as clay and himself as the potter. He molded and sculpted them to conform to an image he considered correct. The third treated his students as if they were plants in his garden. He realized that each flower, tree, and shrub needed the proper but unique balance of light, water, and nutrients. He would not water a cactus as he would a rose, nor would he nurture a seedling as he would a mature tree.

I often think of the teacher-gardener as a metaphor for the role of an effective psychotherapist—a psychologist, clinical social worker, or family therapist. He can act as a strengthened ally for the patient, helping to nurture the patient's own efforts toward health, independence, and fulfillment.

Moreover, each therapeutic experience is so unique that to attempt to simplify and codify how individual patients will respond is truly impossible. Of course, when someone is depressed, there are common themes of abandonment, isolation, and rejection, but exactly how these play themselves out for each person is as unique as a signature. In fact, that's what makes psychology so creative and exciting.

In spite of the uniqueness of each therapeutic relationship, there are some general guidelines that may help you and your loved one establish the therapeutic relationship that will be integral to his recovery from depression.

WHAT TO LOOK FOR IN A GOOD PSYCHOTHERAPIST

People often wonder how to recognize if they are receiving appropriate care from their therapist. Use the following criteria to help you answer that question:

- The psychotherapist must believe that your loved one has the power to overcome his depression. If that faith does not exist—even after a frank discussion about the importance of this belief—then it's time to move on.
- The psychotherapist must attempt to empower you, your loved one, and your family. As the psychiatrist Judith Lewis Herman, who teaches at Harvard Medical School, explains in her book, *Trauma and Recovery,* "No intervention that takes power away from the [patient] can possibly foster her recovery, no matter how much it appears to be in her immediate best interest."

- If your loved one has abdicated responsibility for self-care or threatens to hurt himself or others, the psychotherapist must step in with rapid intervention. Nevertheless, the therapist should consult your loved one as much as possible and offer choices within a framework of safety and caring.
- The therapist should have a clear strategy for helping your loved one regain control over the depression and his life.
- In the absence of adequate familial or social support, the therapist must be willing to act as the strengthened ally with your loved one.
- The therapist should offer objectivity and another point of view. He or she should reframe experiences in a way that promotes your loved one's independence.

As Herman explains, "The therapist's role is both intellectual and relational, fostering both insight and empathic connection." The therapeutic relationship is based on mutual trust-not force, coercion, or control. Therapy that works is a collaborative process.

Often, you don't recognize the impact of the therapeutic relationship at the time. Only on hindsight, when the crisis has passed, and the problems of living that we all face become the focus of the therapeutic interaction, can you see the changes that have been made. In the midst of the storm, you may not have a sense that a safe port exists. The therapist, in collaboration with you and your loved one, will form the core of a team that will fight together to reach that safe port, to reach toward recovery.

TALKING WITH YOUR LOVED ONE'S PSYCHOTHERAPIST

Although the family is an important part of the treatment and recovery team, there are some situations, both therapeutic and ethical/legal, that may make it difficult for you to be involved as much as you would like. Your loved one's therapist will want to empower him by allowing him to retain and maintain as much control as possible over his treatment without betraying his trust, which would undermine his recovery.

All medical and psychological professionals are bound by laws requiring them to preserve the confidentiality of patient-doctor communications. Without express written consent from your loved one, the therapist cannot share any information about his treatment with you.

The laws protecting confidentiality create the proper safe environment for your loved one to discuss in his therapy sessions anything he feels to be important without the threat of disclosure or betrayal.

Until now, I have talked extensively about strategies that you can incorporate to help your loved one fight for recovery from depression. There may be some situations, however, in which less familial involvement is essential. For example, in families where there has been physical, sexual, or emotional abuse, confidentiality is essential.

Finding the right balance between your involvement in the therapy as a strengthened ally and protecting the confidentiality of your loved one who is depressed is a critical aspect of effective therapy. Often the therapist will err on the side of caution to protect the patient until a thorough assessment of the family and personal dynamics is established. This may take longer than any of you would like.

I had one case in which these issues were quite relevant.

My patient Kathy's twenty-three-year-old daughter, Melinda, had recently moved back home after a stormy breakup with her boyfriend. In the month following Melinda's crisis, Kathy became increasingly concerned about her daughter's behavior. She wasn't grooming herself, she wouldn't get out of bed until well after noon, and one evening Kathy discovered her daughter inducing vomiting after dinner.

Kathy called Melinda's therapist, and together, although with some difficulty, they persuaded Melinda to go to the hospital for an evaluation and possible treatment.

Much to Kathy's surprise and distress, the psychiatric team kept her at a distance while they performed this evaluation. And she became even more uneasy when she discovered pages of Melinda's dark, scary, tearstained poetry that she had casually left in the den of their house. Kathy brought this to the hospital, giving it to the psychiatrist in charge. He made little comment, except to ask Kathy, "How did you come upon these writings?"

The psychiatrist's question made Kathy believe that the clinical staff suspected she was responsible for her daughter's depression. She felt that her desire to be helpful had been interpreted as intrusiveness, and this upset her very much. She became angry and defensive with the psychiatrist, and left the hospital in tears. The truth was, Kathy was already harboring guilty feelings about her daughter's condition.

In our work together, we found a way for Kathy to communicate her frustration to the psychiatrist without alienating him. Kathy, the psychiatrist, and I had a three-way conversation about Kathy's concerns and her desire to be helpful without seeming meddlesome. She was able to communicate her fears. In turn, the psychiatrist expressed his need to put together the team's findings in a way that preserved confidentiality. He believed that eventually, Kathy could play an important role in Melinda's recovery.

It took about ten days for the staff to assess Melinda and evaluate Kathy's relationship to her. After that time, the staff members felt that they had found the right balance of individual treatment, proper medication, and a way of including Kathy in family therapy.

For a strengthened ally, hospitalization and waiting can be overwhelming. Having support at this time can be helpful in developing a patient and ultimately helpful attitude.

Therapists have different strategies for dealing with issues of confidentiality. Laws regarding confidentiality are the orienting principle by which all decisions need to be made. These vary from state to state, but in general all states follow certain basic guidelines. Patients own the right of confidentiality, which means that if your loved one is an otherwise competent adult, the therapist must get her written consent to have any conversations with you or anyone else about her diagnosis and treatment. The confidentiality waiver is specific, not general: it applies to certain people for certain periods of time. As a strengthened ally, you may want and need to participate in your loved one's care and have more information on a regular basis. You can ask your loved one to tell the therapist that she would like you to be involved and would like to sign a general release. For this to be possible, your loved one would have to tell the doctor, "Look, it's O.K. to tell my sister anything she wants to know," and then sign a statement to that effect.

The therapist can also initiate the inclusion of family members in the treatment. Since depression often carries with it feelings of rejection, the therapist may want the depressed individual to reach out to family members. He may ask the patient to bring his wife to the session or to call his folks to let them how what's happening with him.

How much gets revealed in a session is also a tricky matter. The therapist may encourage you or your loved one to talk about difficult issues in the session without actually saying anything about them himself. For example, the therapist might say, "If you're feeling rejected because your husband is watching TV in bed at night, this would be important to bring up at our next family session."

There are certain exceptions to these confidentiality rules. The doctor or therapist may break confidentiality without permission if he feels the patient is imminently suicidal. In such a case he is exercising due care to prevent the suicide. "Due care" is usually defined as what any reasonable psychiatrist would do in the same situation. He may choose to hospitalize the patient involuntarily and/or call the patient's family to get them involved in helping prevent the suicide.

Also if a patient threatens to commit an act of violence against a specific person, saying, for example, "I'm going to kill my wife," and the professional believes it to be a genuine threat, in most states he is required to warn the potential victim and the police.

In California and some other states, if a therapist has strong reason to suspect that a patient is abusing an elderly person, a dependent adult, or a child, he has the duty to break confidentiality and report the suspected abuse to local authorities or protective agencies.

If the person being treated is an adolescent or child, the parents are the ultimate holders of the confidentiality unless there has been physical or sexual abuse by the parents. If the teenager reveals drug or alcohol use or sexual activity, the therapist walks a fine line. If these issues need to be talked about because of their links to depression and suicide, I for one prefer the teenager to reveal them to his parents in a session together, rather than my divulging them to the parents and destroying the trust I've established with my patient.

In every situation, the therapist should put the best interests of his patient first.

WHAT TO LOOK FOR IN
PSYCHIATRIC CARE

Just as you pay attention to the kind of psychotherapist your loved one will be working with, so should you have certain criteria for a good psychiatrist. Bear in mind that a good psychiatrist not only has mastery of medications and their side effects but is also compassionate and engaged.

According to Los Angeles–based psychiatrist Dr. Christine Forest, during the first visit the psychiatrist will set the tone of future interactions. She should be supportive, nonjudgmental, and empowering—that is, just like the psychotherapist, she should believe that your loved one *can and will* improve. She'll ask for the chief complaint, though that is not always key to the diagnosis, and she'll identify the spectrum of symptoms. She'll also take a history of symptoms, life events, medical issues, and medications. Finally, she should inquire about substance abuse.

The psychiatrist will make a diagnosis and help your loved one take ownership of it. She'll make a list of problems and prioritize them. She'll set short- and long-term goals for treatment and manage your loved one's expectations about recovery. While doing this, she should engage his commitment and active participation in the treatment plan. He is an active part of the treatment team, not just a passive recipient of care.

Indeed, Dr. Forest defines a good psychiatric relationship as one that is based on mutual respect for one another's contributions to the healing process and on the trust that both parties will hear each other out.

In prescribing treatment, the psychiatrist will want to avoid or offset side effects while using the minimum possible dose of medication. This, as we have seen, can be a matter of trial and error and can take some time. A good psychiatrist will carefully fine-tune the dosage of medication. For instance, Dr. Forest described to me cases in which she prescribed oral solutions of medications that can be taken in tiny dosages for people who are very sensitive— 5 mgs. may be too little, but 7 mgs. may be too much.

Communication between the psychiatrist and your loved one is all-important. This is where you may be able to step in as a strengthened ally. With psychiatric visits sometimes lasting only 15 to 20 minutes, it can be difficult for your loved one to get the kind of attention and care he needs. With his permission, you may accompany him on his visits to the psychiatrist. Be sure to have your questions ready—writing them down often helps you cover the ground you need to. If the medications are having side effects, be sure to list them (and why they're problematic) and ask the psychiatrist to address these concerns. Perhaps a change of dosage or medication will be in order. You may want to take notes during this consultation or even audio tape the visit for future reference.

Your loved one's care may need to be coordinated among several professionals—the psychiatrist, the psychotherapist, the primary care physician, and perhaps a specialist such as an endocrinologist. Your loved one may need to sign releases to allow the psychiatrist to share his personal information with these other members of his health-care team.

It's important for one person to act as the quarterback or coordinator if a team approach is necessary. In my practice, I typically take this role, scheduling conference calls with family members and others on the health-care team as necessary to make sure that we are working together seamlessly. You as a caregiver can be extremely helpful in acting as the liaison among the family, your affected loved one, and the medical team.

It's also important to understand your insurance benefits/exclusions. Medications and psychiatric treatment can be expensive, and some people run out of insurance before their treatment is completed. Sadly, the relapse rate for those who discontinue treatment abruptly can be as high as 80 percent. Clearly, it's important to stay in treatment, even if your loved one has difficulty affording it. But how to accomplish this?

The good news is that psychiatrists are quite familiar with the mental health system and the financial difficulties individuals can face. You might want to bring up insurance issues with the psychiatrist in advance of running out of benefits. Indeed, your loved one may be ashamed to admit that he is low on funds, and being in such a difficult situation can even reinforce the depression. But you can give the physician a call. She may have a sliding scale or know of other programs for low income patients that are subsidized by the pharmaceutical company. She may have samples of medication that she can distribute free of charge. Organizations that provide grants or financial assistance to which your psychiatrist can refer you include the Partnership for Prescription Access and the Patient Access Network Foundation, and Web sites like Together RX access (http://www.togetherrxaccess .com/home.html).

There are ways around these financial issues that will prevent your loved one from falling through the cracks. He may be too immobilized or feel too embarrassed to ask about them, but you can certainly seek some solutions.

Finally, please keep in mind that sometimes we create a false allegiance to a professional. It's perfectly acceptable to seek a second opinion from a different psychiatrist if the advice doesn't sit well or if the doctor-patient fit is uncomfortable. The consulting psychiatrist may reinforce what the first doctor said or may come up with some new solutions that you have yet to try. Compatibility is important in the doctor-patient relationship and helps patients comply with their doctors' orders.

HOSPITALIZATION

Under what circumstances is a depressed person hospitalized? The law states that hospitalization must occur when a depressed individual is a danger to himself or others.

It's important to think of hospitalization not as a punishment but as a way station that places the patient in the least restrictive environment for his safety. Ideally, the patient and the therapist decide that because of the overwhelming nature of the depression, and an imminent threat to his life, the least restrictive environment is the hospital—it is the safest place in which the depressed individual can function without life-threatening consequences.

Hospitalization offers a structured, though at times relatively boring, environment in which treatment occurs on a daily basis. Medication is carefully administered and a team evaluates the progress and prognosis of your loved one. In the hospital environment, time can seem to go extremely slowly.

For you as a strengthened ally, this can be an incredibly stressful period in which the strain of carrying on with your daily routines is added to the worry of how your loved one is progressing. Hospital visits, when permitted, can be quite demanding and strenuous. It may be, though, that hospitalization can create a safe haven for you and your family. You may feel that you don't have to worry as much because you know your loved one is being treated and is safe.

In *Darkness Visible,* William Styron describes the soothing effect hospitalization had on him: "I was amazed to discover that the fantasies of self-destruction all but disappeared within a few days after I checked in, and this again is testimony to the pacifying effect that the hospital can create, its immediate value as a sanctuary where peace can return to the mind."

The hospital may offer patients' family members support groups or family group counseling. These can be quite helpful in allaying your anxiety and sense of isolation. You may also find that you become involved in family therapy sessions with your loved one as his treatment proceeds.

WHEN YOUR LOVED ONE COMES HOME FROM THE HOSPITAL

It can be a tense time when your loved one returns from a hospitalization, especially if he has been hospitalized against his will.

Since my mother refused treatment for her depression, my father and our family doctor devised a plan to hospitalize her, supposedly for "tests" for a preexisting physical condition. Once in the hospital, when she discovered the true nature of their plan, she became enraged. She felt betrayed and blamed me, my father, the doctors, the hospital—everyone—for her mistreatment and humiliation.

After her release, we all pretended that she was coming home from a hospital stay for physical illness, when we all knew it was a failed attempt to deal with her emotional state. The phrase "walking on eggshells" doesn't come close to describing the fragility of our guarded exchanges. The tension in our house was palpable, unbearable. It crackled in the air like thousands of volts of electricity.

But your experience doesn't have to be like that. Remembering that time I have often thought, again, "If only I had known . . ." The issues of my mother's depression should have been addressed more directly, and of course, the modern medications used today were yet to be developed.

There is no point in your loved one coming home unless the chances of his success at resisting depression are reasonably high. Let the psychiatric team know that you will be taking over the care at home and would like to be involved in the discharge planning and exit interviews. Plans need to be in place so that everyone knows what to expect, including

- when the appointment for the next office visit is
- what the medication schedule is and what side effects, if any, to expect

- plans for your loved one to go back to work
- how to talk with others about what has happened
- how to deal with children in the house (this might be a good time for a family meeting)

You may also need to expend some effort helping your loved one reintegrate into social life. Often people don't know what to say when they learn that someone has just been released from a psychiatric facility. If a friend comes to you asking how your loved one is doing, there's no point in keeping a secret. However, you can set limits for how much you and your loved one want to talk about the experience.

Don't let family or friends ignore or abandon your loved one just because they feel awkward. Let them know how to act. Tell them how you want them to treat your loved one. Let friends know that you are speaking for yourself and your needs, and that it's more than O.K. to talk with your loved one—you don't have to be your loved one's spokesperson.

It might be helpful for you and your loved one to rehearse a response to others' confusion or discomfort. You may decide together how you are going to talk about the hospitalization. For example, you might tell others, "This has been tough on all of us. It's O.K. to ask Charlie about his stay in the hospital, but he only wants to talk about it for ten or fifteen minutes at a time. He told me he prefers to focus on enjoying his life now, doing normal things." Or you might say, "I'm not in the mood to talk about this now. Check with Charlie and see where he's at. I don't want to speak for him."

Your loved one might have given up some control over his life while in the hospital. Encourage him to regain and maintain as much control as is now reasonable. It may be useful for him to make a list of the areas in which he has lost control and go over with him what he can take back for himself.

Use hopeful words in communicating with your loved one about the situation. References to the depression as "devastating" or "catastrophic" can only lead to despair. Don't go into denial, but do pay attention to and validate improvements and little victories. Be sure you express love and appreciation. You might say, for example, "We're glad you're home now, Charlie. We've missed you. The first few days home may be uncomfortable, but let's keep talking to get through this time together. It's an adjustment for all of us."

It's also important to have realistic expectations. Although the crisis has passed, your loved one may still have depressive episodes. How to handle them should be part of your exit interviews and continuing treatment plans with the hospital's psychiatric staff.

Expect mixed feelings. You will experience excitement as well as fear. It's useful to talk about both.

THE FINANCIAL BURDEN

For five years, I saw the Rose family—Jane; her husband, Stan; and their three young daughters—for free. Jane had been diagnosed with cancer. Her many treatments and disabilities had caused her to taper and eventually give up her lucrative law career. The medical bills were enormous, and the family's financial needs were great; yet I could not let the Roses traverse this difficult terrain without psychological support from me. When Jane died, I continued to help her family adjust to its terrible loss, again at no cost to them.

A small portion of my practice is devoted to cases such as that of the Rose family. And I know that from time to time, most of my colleagues have provided services for free (pro bono) too.

Of course, there are limits to what an individual therapist is able or willing to do, but there are therapists, clinics, and agencies that are capable of providing reduced-fee or no-fee services during a crisis.

Not being able to afford therapy does not have to stop you from getting help for your loved one. As a strengthened ally, you can ask for a fee reduction. It is reasonable, if a genuine need exists, to negotiate a reduced fee and a repayment schedule. If the therapist cannot manage reducing the fee, in all likelihood he or she will refer you to someone who can. This may be a laborious, time-consuming experience, but it is possible to get some financial relief. In Appendix 2, I list many organizations whose primary purpose is to help your loved one get the help he needs.

Hospitalization is expensive—there is no way around that. With adequate insurance, however, it can be made manageable. Unfortunately, however, most insurance companies do not cover mental illnesses as completely as they do "physical" illnesses—although, as we have seen, illnesses such as depression often have physiological origins.

All of us in the mental health professions hope that soon this will change. Influential people like Rosalynn Carter and Tipper Gore have been working tirelessly to guarantee that mental illnesses achieve parity with physical illnesses in the eyes of the insurance companies, and they have met with some success. Lifetime benefit caps for mental and physical illnesses are now equal.

In the meantime, as a strengthened ally, you can join forces with others who find themselves in the same situation as you. Organizations like NAMI and the National Mental Health Association, with chapters all over the country, advocate for parity and an end to stigma. With your voice added to the rest, perhaps this inequity will finally be eradicated.

◆

CHAPTER 12

When Depression Can Be Dangerous

I WAS TWENTY-TWO YEARS OLD AND A FIRST-YEAR JU-nior high school reading and literature teacher when I met Jennifer. She was one of my students. She died at the age of fourteen, a victim of suicide.

I learned about Jennifer's death only after she had moved away. But I knew she was depressed because she would write poetry—not just any kind of poetry, but wonderfully lyrical free verse with profound metaphors. It seemed a mixture of Edgar Allan Poe and Bob Dylan, dark but hauntingly beautiful and philosophical. She was the type of student a teacher cherished, someone who loved to learn, and was yearning, eager to create.

Over the summer, she called me at home—I never learned how she got my number—to thank me for all I had taught her about metaphors and all that I had tried to do for her. "I'm running away," she said with sad finality. She had been living with her elderly grandparents, who did not understand her sense of isolation or appreciate the seriousness of her depression.

"Why don't you come by summer school to see me tomorrow?" I asked. "Maybe I can get you some help."

"It's too late," she replied. "I already left. I'm calling from a phone booth and just want to say good-bye."

I tried to keep her on the phone, but she said she had to go. I never found out exactly what happened, but I did learn that she died sometime later that summer, and by the way it was said, the unspoken truth was that she had killed herself. I learned later from her friends that she had had an "accident" and had died from a drug overdose.

There is no question that Jennifer's death had a profound impact on me. Coupled with my experiences with my mother, it convinced me to become a trainee at the Los Angeles Suicide Prevention Center. This led to the meeting with the director of the Los Angeles center that changed my life forever. At the end of that year of training and hot-line work, I wrote my master's thesis, "Adolescent Suicide—Assault on Isolation," and I decided to continue on for a doctorate and become a clinical psychologist.

What I learned from that research and the years with the Los Angeles Suicide Prevention Center is that most and perhaps all suicides can be prevented. With enough intervention, the will to live can heal and overcome the impulse to die.

YOUNG LIVES LOST

In reflecting upon Jennifer's life and her untimely death, I have often thought, "If only I had known the signs. Maybe I could have done something . . . maybe I could have saved her."

The memory of Jennifer's suicide so many years ago returned forcefully when I read a *Los Angeles Times* report on a tragic double suicide in the fashionable Los Angeles suburb of Rancho Palos Verdes. Two teenagers, sixteen-year-old Chris Mills and his fifteen-year-old girlfriend, Heidi Chamberlain, jumped from a cliff high above the pounding surf.

Outwardly the pair had seemed well adjusted. Chris was an A and B student, taking a full courseload of college-level classes. He had just found his first job pumping gas. To many he seemed happy and outgoing. Heidi loved horseback riding and soccer. Her friends had described her as "passionate and lively." Religion had recently become an important part of her life.

So what went wrong? The journalists J. Michael Kennedy and Jeff Leeds write, "As any adolescent can tell you, the parents are sometimes the last to know the inner workings of lost young souls. And on the barricaded cliff from which the two children leaped to their deaths . . . their young friends said that, in hindsight, it was clear that the couple's world had a troubled underside."

Chris's closest friends had noticed that he seemed obsessed with death. "He was kind of death-happy," one buddy said. Another friend said that he would talk about how depressed he got, "but I never thought he would go this far." Chris had turned in a creative-writing assignment on suicide and had wept on hearing of the self-inflicted death of the rock star Kurt Cobain.

For her part, Heidi was described as a highly volatile young woman who tended to "dramatize" her life. Shortly before her death, she had argued with her parents about the rules they had established regarding her relationship with her new boyfriend.

As so many of the friends and relatives of this couple grieved, the salient theme arising from their confusion and tears was that "this didn't have to happen." There were warning signs—warning signs that everyone wished they had taken more seriously.

As with Jennifer's death, this tragic story of warning signs unheeded made me realize how little has changed in the hearts and minds of caregivers wishing they had another chance to undo the impossible when someone attempts or commits suicide. The goal of this chapter is to remind you that tragedies such as Jennifer's death more than thirty years ago and Chris and Heidi's more recently don't have to happen. *There are warning signs, and when you recognize them, there are things you can do to prevent a loved one's suicide.*

READING THE SIGNS

As the psychiatrist David D. Burns makes clear in his book, *Feeling Good*, "Although suicidal thoughts are common even in individuals who are not depressed, the occurrence of a suicidal impulse if you *are* depressed is always to be regarded as a dangerous symptom." But how do you recognize a suicidal impulse in another person? The following clues may help:

- Your loved one loses interest in activities and hobbies that were sources of pleasure and is disinterested in her work or career.
- Your loved one gives away favorite possessions—stamp collections, jewelry, money, and so on.
- Your loved one writes a will.
- She has conversations that seem rational but have an unusually dark quality to them in which death is ennobled

or elevated. (For example, Chris Mills had said, "The other side is gonna be so much more fun.")

- She makes oblique references to others who have died that, although the death may have been tragic, communicate a sense of identification or commiseration with the victim. For example, Chris seemed to identify with Kurt Cobain.
- She begins writing poetry or prose laced with darkness, images of death, and profound loneliness.
- She continuously and persistently discounts the positive and embraces the negative.
- There is an increase in alcohol or drug abuse.
- She makes preparations and/or talks about a suicide plan that is concrete, specific, within her means, and lethal, and there are no deterrents to her carrying out the plan. It is a myth that people who talk about suicide don't actually follow through! Talking about suicide is a sign of great danger!
- She seems detached from her emotions and withdraws from friends or family.

In addition to these signs, it's helpful to be aware of factors that may put your loved one at greater risk for suicide. These include:

- A history of depression or other mental illness. According to Dr. Jan Fawcett, the chairman of the department of psychiatry at Rush-Presbyterian–St. Luke's Medical Center in Chicago, 93 to 95 percent of suicides suffer from a psychiatric illness (most commonly depression), substance abuse associated with depression, or schizophrenia.
- A history of previous suicide attempts.
- A family history of suicide.
- Marital status: Those at greatest risk are unmarried and childless. Next in descending order of risk come those

who are widowed, separated or divorced, married with no children, and married with children.

- A major career failure such as job loss or business bankruptcy.
- Lawyers, psychiatrists, policemen, and musicians have higher suicide rates than the general public.
- Gender: Women make more attempts at suicide, but men are more likely to succeed. Men often use more lethal, violent means to end their lives such as shooting or hanging versus drug overdoses.
- Age: Suicide risk tends to increase with age. According to Dr. Mark S. Gold of the Medical School of the University of Florida, the rate for those over the age of sixty-five is fifteen times greater than for the general public. Perhaps this is related to surviving the death of a spouse and/or one's own deteriorating health.
- Health status: Those who are suffering from chronic pain or a terminal illness are at higher risk. A recent major surgery also increases the risk.
- Substance abuse: According to Dr. Jan Fawcett, those who are successful in their suicide attempts have a higher rate of substance abuse. In *On the Edge of Darkness,* Kathy Cronkite quotes him as saying, "[The use of] alcohol plus other substances like marijuana or coke increases the risk [of a successful suicide attempt] by ten times."
- A lifting of the depression: Ironically, those who are pulling out of depression can be at greater risk for suicide than those in a deep depression. The lethargy inherent in depression may have dissipated but left behind suicidal thoughts. At this stage, a depressed individual has more energy to carry out a lethal plan.
- Intense feelings of hopelessness, paranoia, or anxiety. According to unpublished research reported by a Los Ange-

les psychiatrist, Stuart Wolman, anxiety coupled with depression increases the individual's risk for suicide. Dr. Jan Fawcett supports these findings: "Many people who kill themselves develop tremendous anxiety and panic attacks prior to suicide. They are in severe psychic pain; the pain of going on is too excruciating to tolerate."

Perhaps the most important advice I can give you in determining whether your loved one is suicidal is to use your intuition. If you sense that something is wrong, it probably is. Trust your instincts. You're much better off being overly concerned than regretting having missed the signs when it's too late.

Cheryl's fifteen-year-old daughter was exhibiting signs of depression, even suicidal tendencies, after her boyfriend's death in a car accident. Kelly was angry and acting out. Her previously stellar grades had slipped toward C's. She dyed her hair purple and ran away from home twice. She spoke of body piercing and tattoos. Most of the time she seemed sullen and withdrawn.

Cheryl was concerned about Kelly's therapist's more casual attitude. "We'll continue watching it, but this is well within the range of normal adolescent behavior," the therapist said. "It's predictable after losing a boyfriend under such circumstances at this age."

But Cheryl wouldn't buy that. In her gut she knew that Kelly was troubled—more troubled than she had ever seen her. She found herself waking in the middle of the night, worried and anxious about Kelly's well-being. She knew that her daughter's hostility was a sign of deep unhappiness. She became convinced that it was *more than* a sign of teenage angst—it was outright dangerous. Talk therapy didn't seem to be enough.

With her daughter's permission, Cheryl decided to sit in on a therapy session with her daughter to share her concerns. When Kelly saw that her mom was taking her unhappiness seriously, that she wasn't dismissing it, she felt she had room to express her suicidal thoughts. She saw no point in living; she talked about wanting to "join Kevin in heaven." The therapist, upon learning the depth of Kelly's despair, took immediate action and referred Kelly to a psychiatrist for a medical evaluation and treatment with antidepressant medication.

Cheryl trusted her instincts, and she was right. Perhaps in so doing she saved her daughter's life.

STEPPING IN

In the years that I worked at the Los Angeles Suicide Prevention Center, it was branded into my brain time and again that most people—despite their suicidality—don't want to die. Given proper treatment and support, they can get through the period when they are most likely to commit violence to themselves.

Most calls to a suicide prevention center are desperate attempts to get past immediate unbearable pain. Just the act of talking with a counselor who really listens and who has a strategy for follow-up care gets most suicidal individuals over the darkest moments.

A letter to the editor in *The New York Times* brought this point home to me yet again. The writer of the letter, Kenneth M. Glatt, is the commissioner of mental hygiene in Dutchess County, New York. He described how in an earlier news article, residents of San Francisco had argued against the erection of barriers in addition to a suicide patrol at the Golden Gate Bridge because they believed, "People who wanted to commit suicide would simply find another way to do it."

He refutes this belief, explaining that experience on the Mid-Hudson Bridge at Poughkeepsie demonstrates that would-be jumpers are ambivalent about dying right up to the last minute. They will reach out for help if it is made available to them. He writes: "On the bridge there are two call boxes which proclaim that

'Life is worth living,' and 'Help is available 24 hours a day.' " These boxes connect directly to a county mental health hot line. "In 11 years, the phones have been used 55 times," he continues. "In only one instance did a caller jump, and this represents the only suicide on record of the 50 people taken from the bridge to a local emergency room."

Glatt makes clear that suicidal behavior is usually time-limited, frequently impulsive, and often fueled by alcohol and drugs. When the warning signs are present, as a strengthened ally you must find the courage to respond to your intuition and seek help.

I want to be very clear on this issue: Suicidal feelings in a depressed individual are an indication of the need for more treatment. Suicide is not a solution to depression—treatment is! You are no longer in a wait-and-see situation! Your loved one's suicide attempt or even a seemingly rational discussion of a suicide plan is not just a cry for help—it's a call to action!

STEPS TO TAKE

The things you say and do when you believe a suicide attempt is imminent can be vital to your loved one's survival. Adhere to the following steps when possible.

Say:

- "I know things look hopeless right now, and I'm taking this very seriously. We need to get help."
- "Suicide is not the answer. More help is!"
- "You or I need to call the psychologist/psychiatrist and we both need to talk to him."
- "I'm here with you and I'm not going to leave. You are not alone."
- "We are going to the hospital right away."

If there is resistance to these steps:

- Call your local suicide prevention center or similar hot line.
- Call 911 or the police. Police departments in some cities have psychiatric emergency teams (PET). These trained therapists will come to your home to do an immediate assessment.
- If there is no PET in your community, the emergency workers or police will come with an ambulance to transport your loved one to the hospital for evaluation.

These measures are all necessary because most suicidal individuals *do not want to die.*

◆

As a strengthened ally, you want to have as few regrets as possible. I wish it were possible to guarantee that your efforts would prevent a suicide attempt. Unfortunately, sometimes it's not possible, no matter what you do. What I have learned from caregivers who have survived the suicide of a loved one—as painful and devastating as that is—is that eventually it is possible to find some solace.

Karen, whose husband had committed suicide, told me some time afterward, "Even though there can be no erasing of the pain, it is somehow oddly possible to accept that I did everything in my power. And once you do that, what more can you say or do? In a strange way there is comfort in that inner knowledge because no one can take that away."

CHAPTER 13

Finding
a New Normal

Some years ago, as the national clinical director
of The Wellness Community, I was on a site visit to the Boston
facility. As mentioned earlier, The Wellness Community is a free
program of psychological and emotional support for cancer
patients and their families. I was sitting in on a family-member
group discussion.

At one point, a woman named Diane, discussing her husband's
fight for recovery from leukemia, said, "You know, for a while there
I was afraid that if the leukemia wasn't going to get Fred, the depression would."

Diane explained with much relief that this moment in time, with Fred's leukemia in remission and the depression lifting, was sweet and happy. "It's as if we've come through a great battle together," she said.

And then she paused and took a deep breath. "You know," she confided softly, "things aren't really the same. It's not quite like it was. It's normal—but you know, really, it's a *new* normal. Our lives have flown apart in so many directions and have just now gotten put together. It's like a rubber band having been stretched to its limit. It still works, but it's a little loose around the edges."

The group laughed in recognition.

HEALING

In my years working as a psychologist, I have encountered so many family members and their depressed loved ones who have said, "I can't wait for things to return to the way they were." But really, how can they be exactly the same? *60 Minutes*'s Mike Wallace has said about recovering from his bout with depression, "Little by little, it heals; it knits, and it's better. Maybe it leaves a little bit of a scar . . ."

As a strengthened ally, you will always have a worry deep in the back of your mind, "Could this happen again? Am I prepared to deal with it? Are we?" But the greatest source of comfort is the knowledge that if you've gotten through it once, you can get through it again. Strengthened allies learn to use these challenges, these scars marking difficulties overcome, as profound sources of empowerment and connection to their loved ones.

Of course, there are no simple answers. Time and time again, my work with cancer patients has shown me that when they talk of surviving this dread disease and their fight for recovery, they describe the secondary gains—and at times the perverse benefits—they've derived from coming through the illness. And then they ask themselves, "Did I have to have cancer in my life to learn these lessons?"

The answer is no. But the solutions and coping strategies they've acquired as a result of the illness remain emblazoned in their hearts and minds. Some of these cancer survivors talk about learning to say no, to set limits with family and friends; others make career and/or relationship changes.

Yet despite the many difficulties in their lives, all tell of the same resolve. Things are not the same since the disease struck. But, perhaps surprisingly, they don't want to go back to the way things were before. Like Diane, they have found a *new normal*—a new way of living that, the challenges notwithstanding, is better.

Those recovering from depression experience a similar process. In reflecting on the many depression memoirs that have been written in recent years, I could see that, like heroes returning from battle, the writers gave testimonials to the value of life. All of them have learned to reframe this horrific experience and to find some good in it—some way in which they have grown and been changed.

William Styron quotes the first several lines of Dante's *Inferno*—"In the middle of the journey of our life, I found myself in a dark wood, For I had lost my path"—to describe his experience of depression. He later compares his recovery with Dante's emergence from Hell:

> For those who have dwelt in depression's dark wood, and known its inexplicable agony, their return from the abyss is not unlike the ascent of the poet, trudging upward and upward out of hell's black depths and at last emerging into what he saw as "the shining world." There, whoever has been restored to health has almost always been restored to the capacity for serenity and joy.

Throughout the many memoirs, depression is often compared to losing one's way in the dark. And once the depression lifts, renewal and hope return. Whenever I witness such a return to life, I find myself unconsciously humming the song "Amazing Grace" and thinking of all those whom I have known—including my mother—who have battled depression.

Toward the end of my humming I land on the line "I once was lost but now am found. . . ." I remember all those who have overcome their depression and feel tremendous gratitude. Kay Redfield Jamison writes in *An Unquiet Mind,* "After each seeming death within my mind or heart, love has returned to re-create hope and to restore life."

FORGIVENESS

Throughout this book I have woven stories from my experiences with my mother and father. There is one last story that remains frozen in time and in my memory. It occurred on October 9, 1989, four and a half years before my mother's death from complications from a series of strokes.

The date is clear in my mind because of several events that coalesced then. First, it was my forty-third birthday. It was also Yom Kippur, the Jewish Day of Atonement, the holiest day of the year. The rabbi of our temple had asked me to lead an afternoon seminar entitled "Pathways to Forgiveness: Explorations of Guilt and Repentance." My mother, after her first stroke had left her partially paralyzed, decided to come with us to pray and also to listen to her son teach on such a holy day. My in-laws, wife, and first cousin and her husband—the family closest to me who had witnessed firsthand many of the experiences I've shared throughout this book—would also be present.

On this auspicious and meaningful day, I went through my presentation. A forgiveness ritual is an important part of the customs associated with Yom Kippur. I facilitated a guided imagery experience in which I suggested that each participant in his or her imagination ask for and receive forgiveness or accept a request for forgiveness from someone in their lives—whichever seemed the most appropriate.

Toward the end of the exercise, I asked who would like to share their experience—the situation for which they were seeking forgiveness or for which they felt guilty. Some people shared deep wounds or actions that had occurred for which they had deep regrets. I could see the sharing of these stories with others brought everyone closer. Tears were shed. Loved ones hugged each other.

Near the very end, my mother stood up, using her walker, and in her somewhat garbled but still coherent voice said, "How can I feel guilty after having raised such a wonderful son like you? What more could a mother want?"

My mother slowly sat down and all those dear to me shared heartfelt glances and began to cry.

There was no more to be said. After a lifetime of struggle, and at times anguish, I was flooded with gratitude at having lived long enough to see the day that my mother would be at peace with herself and her life.

As a strengthened ally, I wish each of you such a moment. And, if that moment has not yet arrived, perhaps my mother's simple statement will help to carry you through the uncertain times until it does.

Books and Resources You May Find Helpful

Beck, Aaron. *Love Is Never Enough*. New York: Harper & Row, 1988.

Burns, David D. *Feeling Good: The New Mood Therapy*. New York: Avon Books, 1992.

——. *The Feeling Good Handbook*. Revised edition. New York: Plume, 1999.

Carter, Rosalynn, with Susan K. Golant. *Helping Yourself Help Others: A Book for Caregivers*. New York: Times Books, 1996.

——. *Helping Someone with Mental Illness*. New York: Times Books, 1999.

Cronkite, Kathy. *On the Edge of Darkness: Conversations About Conquering Depression*. New York: Delta Books, 1994.

Dowling, Collette. *You Mean I Don't Have to Feel This Way? New Help/or Depression, Anxiety, and Addiction*. New York: Bantam Books, 1993.

Duke, Patty, and Gloria Hochman. *A Brilliant Madness: Living with Manic Depressive Illness*. New York: Bantam Books, 1993.

Gold, Mark S. *The Good News About Depression*. New York: Bantam Books, 1995.

Goleman, Daniel. *Emotional Intelligence*. New York: Bantam Books, 1995.

Greist, John H., and James W. Jefferson. *Depression and Its Treatment*. Rev. ed. Washington, D.C.: American Psychiatric Press, 1992.

Heckler, Richard A. *Waking Up Alive: The Descent, the Suicide Attempt, and the Return to Life*. New York: Ballantine Books, 1994.

Herman, Judith Lewis. *Trauma and Recovery.* New York: Basic Books, 1992.

Jamison, Kay Redfield. *An Unquiet Mind: A Memoir of Moods and Madness.* New York: Knopf, 1995.

Kramer, Peter D. *Listening to Prozac.* New York: Viking Penguin, 1993.

Ornish, Dean. *Love & Survival: The Scientific Basis for the Healing Power of Intimacy.* New York: Harper Collins, 1998.

Oster, Gerald D., and Sarah S. Montgomery. *Helping Your Depressed Teenager: A Guide for Parents and Caregivers.* New York: John Wiley & Sons, 1995.

Podell, Ronald M., with Porter Shimer. *Contagious Emotions: Staying Well When Your Loved One Is Depressed.* New York: Pocket Books, 1992.

Pollin, Irene, with Susan K. Golant. *Taking Charge: How to Master the Eight Most Common Fears of Long-Term Illness.* New York: Times Books, 1996.

Polonsky, William H. *Diabetes Burnout: What to Do When You Can't Take It Anymore.* Alexandria, Va.: American Diabetes Association, 1999.

Ross, Jerilyn. *Triumph Over Fear: A Book of Help and Hope for People with Anxiety, Panic Attacks, and Phobias.* New York: Bantam Books, 1994.

Seligman, Martin. *Learned Optimism: How to Change Your Mind and Your Life.* New York: Pocket Books, 1990.

Somer, Elizabeth. *Food and Mood: The Complete Guide to Eating Well and Feeling Your Best.* New York: Henry Holt, 1995.

Styron, William. *Darkness Visible: A Memoir of Madness.* New York: Random House, 1990.

Thiboldeaux, Kim and Mitch Golant. *The Total Cancer Wellness Guide: Reclaiming Your Life After Diagnosis.* Dallas, Tx.: Benbella Books, 2007.

Wurtzel, Elizabeth. *Prozac Nation: Young and Depressed in America.* New York: Riverhead Books, 1995.

Books on Visualization and Relaxation

Benson, Herbert. The *Relaxation Response.* New York: Avon Books, 1975.

Gawain, Shakti. *Creative Visualization.* New York: Bantam Books, 1995.

Samuels, Mike. *Seeing with the Mind's Eye.* New York: Random House, 1975.

◆

Organizations You May Find Helpful

Information Clearinghouses

NATIONAL CLEARINGHOUSE FOR ALCOHOL AND DRUG INFORMATION
P.O. Box 2345
Rockville, MD 20847-2345
(301) 468-2600
(800) 729-6686
www.ncadi.samhsa.gov

NATIONAL MENTAL HEALTH CONSUMER'S SELF-HELP CLEARINGHOUSE
1211 Chestnut Street, Suite 1207
Philadelphia, PA 19107
(215) 751-1810
(800) 553-4539
www.mhselfhelp.org

National Organizations Dealing with Depression and Bipolar Illness

AMERICAN ACADEMY OF CHILD AND ADOLESCENT PSYCHIATRY
3615 Wisconsin Avenue NW
Washington, D.C. 20016
(202) 966-7300
www.aacap.org

AMERICAN ASSOCIATION OF SUICIDOLOGY
5221 Wisconsin Avenue, NW
Washington, D.C. 20015
(800) 273-TALK (8255)
www.suicidology.org

AMERICAN PSYCHIATRIC ASSOCIATION
1000 Wilson Boulevard, Suite 1825
Arlington, VA 22209-3901
www. psych.org

AMERICAN PSYCHOLOGICAL ASSOCIATION
750 1st Street NE
Washington, D.C. 20036
(202) 336-5500
www.apa.org

DEPRESSION AFTER DELIVERY/POSTPARTUM SUPPORT INTERNATIONAL
P.O. Box 60931
Santa Barbara, CA 93160
(800) 944-4773
www.postpartum.net

LITHIUM INFORMATION CENTER
Information Centers
Madison Institute of Medicine
7617 Mineral Point Road, Suite 300
Madison, WI 53717
(608) 827-2470
www.miminc.org

National Alliance for the Mentally Ill (NAMI)
Colonial Place Three
2107 Wilson Boulevard, Suite 300
Arlington, VA 22201
(703) 524-7600
(800) 950-NAMI
www.nami.org

National Depressive and Manic Depressive Association
730 N. Franklin, Suite 501
Chicago, IL 60610
(800) 826-3632
www.ndmda.org

National Institute of Mental Health (NIMH)
Depression Awareness, Recognition and Treatment (D/ART) Program
5600 Fishers Lane
Rockville, MD 20857
(800) 421-4211
www.nimh.nih.gov

National Mental Health Association/Mental Health America
2000 N. Beauregard Street, 6th floor
Alexandria, VA 22311
(800) 969-NMHA
www.nmha.org

National Organization for Seasonal Affective Disorder
P.O. Box 40133
Washington, D.C. 20016
www.nosad.org

Organizations in Related Areas

AGING

ADMINISTRATION ON AGING
  U.S. Health & Human Services
  200 Independence Avenue SW
  Washington, D.C. 20201
  (202) 619-0257
  www.aoa.gov

AMERICAN ASSOCIATION OF RETIRED PERSONS (AARP)
  601 E Street NW
  Washington, D.C. 20049
  (888) 687-2277
  www.aarp.org

AIDS

AIDS HOTLINE
  (800) 342-AIDS
  www.AIDSHotline.org

U.S. DEPARTMENT OF HEALTH AND HUMAN SERVICES
  www.aids.gov

ALZHEIMER'S DISEASE

ALZHEIMER'S ASSOCIATION
  225 N. Michigan Avenue, Fl. 17
  Chicago, IL 60601
  (800) 272-3900
  www.alz.org

ANXIETY AND PANIC DISORDERS

ANXIETY DISORDERS ASSOCIATION OF AMERICA
  (240) 485-1001
  www.adaa.org

CANCER

AMERICAN CANCER SOCIETY
1599 Clifton Road NE
Atlanta, GA 30329
(800) 227-2345
www.cancer.org

THE WELLNESS COMMUNITY–NATIONAL
919 18th Street NW, Suite 54
Washington, D.C. 20006
(202) 659-9709
(800) 793-WELL
www.thewellnesscommunity.org

CHRONIC FATIGUE SYNDROME/EPSTEIN-BARR

CFIDS ASSOCIATION
704-365-2343
www.cfids.org

DIABETES

AMERICAN DIABETES ASSOCIATION
P.O. Box 25757
1701 Beauregard St.
Alexandria, VA 22311
(800) 342-2383
www.diabetes.org

HEART DISEASE

MENDED HEARTS
c/o American Heart Association
7272 Greenville Avenue
Dallas, TX 75231
(800) 242-8721
www.mendedhearts.org
www.americanheart.org

OBSESSIVE COMPULSIVE DISORDER

OBSESSIVE COMPULSIVE ANONYMOUS
P.O. Box 215
New Hyde Park, NY 11040
(516) 739-0662
members.aol.com/west24th/

OBSESSIVE COMPULSIVE FOUNDATION
676 State Street
New Haven, CT 06511
(203) 401-2070
www.ocfoundation.org

PARKINSON'S DISEASE

NATIONAL PARKINSON FOUNDATION
1501 NW Ninth Avenue
Miami, FL 33136
(800) 327-4545
www.parkinson.org

AMERICAN PARKINSON DISEASE ASSOCIATION
135 Parkinson Avenue
Staten Island, NY 10305
(800) 223-2732
www.dpdaparkinson.org

STROKE

NATIONAL INSTITUTE OF NEUROLOGICAL DISORDERS AND STROKE
P.O. Box 5801
Bethesda, MD 20892
(800) 352-9424
www.ninds.nih.gov

STROKE ASSOCIATION
c/o American Heart Association
7272 Greenville Avenue
Dallas, TX 75231
(800) 242-8721
www.strokeassociation.org

SUBSTANCE ABUSE

AL-ANON/ALATEEN
(888) 425-2666
www.al-anon.alateen.org

ALCOHOLICS ANONYMOUS WORLD SERVICES
(212) 870-3400
www.alcoholics-anonymous.org

COCAINE ANONYMOUS WORLD SERVICES
(310) 559-5833
(800) 347-8998 *for meeting locations*
www.ca.org

COCAINE HOTLINE
(800) COCAINE

SUBSTANCE ABUSE AND MENTAL HEALTH SERVICES ADMINISTRATION
1 Choke Cherry Road
Rockville, MD 20857
www.samhsa.gov

NATIONAL MENTAL HEALTH INFORMATION CENTER
www.mentalhealth.samhsa.gov

PRESCRIPTION ASSISTANCE

PARTNERSHIP FOR PRESCRIPTION ACCESS
(800) 4PPA-NOW
www.pparx.org

Together RX Access
www.togetherrxaccess.com

OTHER HELPFUL WEB SITES

Daily Strength.com
www.dailystrength.com

Patient Advocate Foundation
www.patientadvocate.org

Glossary

ADDICTION: A strong physiological or psychological dependence on a chemical substance. When the substance is removed, the individual experiences withdrawal symptoms. Narcotics, alcohol, and sedatives may produce addiction.

ALCOHOLISM: A chronic illness whose symptoms include compulsive, repetitive drinking that impairs one's health and one's social and economic functioning.

ALZHEIMER'S DISEASE: A progressive, irreversible illness that usually occurs later in life. It is characterized by a loss of brain cells and leads to impaired mental functioning.

ANTIDEPRESSANTS: Medications that prevent and/or relieve symptoms of depression. They can return an individual to the emotional state he or she experienced before becoming depressed. Antidepressants include benzodiazepines, beta-blockers, monoamine oxidase inhibitors (MAOIs), selective serotonin reuptake inhibitors (SSRIs), and cyclics.

ATTENTION DEFICIT DISORDER (ADD): A childhood disorder whose symptoms can persist into adulthood. ADD is characterized by a short attention span and difficulty concentrating. It is often treated with stimulants such as Ritalin or antidepressants.

ATYPICAL DEPRESSION: A kind of depression typified by excessive sleepiness (ten or more hours a day), increased appetite, and weight gain. Those with atypical depression can be cheerful as a result of positive events. However, they are also highly sensitive to rejection.

BIPOLAR DISORDER: A major mood disorder also know as **manic depression.** Individuals with this disorder cycle between periods of excessive activity and euphoria (mania) and severe depression. It is believed to be caused by a chemical imbalance in the brain and is often treated with lithium coupled with psychotherapy.

COGNITIVE THERAPY: A treatment method developed by Aaron Beck and based on the theory that how one thinks about issues in one's life can impact one's emotions. (Negative attitudes can cause depression.) Treatment includes the challenging of habitual patterns of thought.

CONFIDENTIALITY: A tenet of providing care that requires psychologists, psychiatrists, and other mental health and medical professionals to maintain patients' privacy.

DELUSION: A false belief that one holds despite overwhelming evidence to the contrary. Delusions can occur when depression is quite severe.

DEPRESSION: A mood disorder that, in its most serious form, can include a variety of physical and emotional symptoms including insomnia, loss of appetite, confusion, slowness, diminished sex drive, and pessimistic, negative emotions.

DYSTHYMIA: Chronic down mood that lasts for at least two years. The periods of depression are shorter, less severe, and less impairing than in major depression.

ELECTROCONVULSIVE THERAPY (ECT): The application of a mild electrical current to the brain to help alleviate the disabling symptoms of severe depression. It is especially useful for older patients with multiple disabilities or those who cannot tolerate or don't respond to antidepressant medications. Anesthetics and muscle relaxants protect patients receiving ECT from pain and injury.

HYPOMANIA: An elevated expansive or irritable mood associated with bipolar illness that is not severe enough to cause a disturbance in an individual's functioning.

LITHIUM CARBONATE: A salt compound used in the treatment of bipolar disorder. Effective in 70 percent of cases. (Carbamazepine and valproate are prescribed to those for whom lithium is ineffective.)

MONOAMINE OXIDASE INHIBITORS (MAOI): A frequently prescribed class of antidepressants. Certain dietary restrictions must be observed when on this medication. MAOIs include medications with the brand names Nardil, Parnate, and Marplan.

NEUROTRANSMITTER: A chemical that circulates in the nervous system and facilitates the transmission of electrical impulses from one nerve cell to the next. Noradrenaline, dopamine, and serotonin are neurotransmitters.

PARKINSON'S DISEASE: A nervous-system disorder believed to result from a depletion of dopamine, a neurotransmitter. Symptoms can include tremors, rigid expression, difficulty walking, slowness of physical and mental responses, and depression.

PSYCHOSIS: A major mental disorder that can accompany severe depression. Symptoms include: disorganization of personality, regressive behavior, inappropriate moods and expressions, delusions, hallucinations, and diminished impulse control.

RAPID CYCLING BIPOLAR ILLNESS: A severe form of bipolar illness in which the individual moves from mania to depression from day to day or even from hour to hour.

SELECTIVE SEROTONIN REUPTAKE INHIBITORS (SSRI): A relatively new class of antidepressants that help to maintain higher levels of the neurotransmitter serotonin in the blood. SSRIs include medications with the brand names Prozac, Zoloft, Paxil, Effexor, Serzone, Desyrel, Asendin, and Wellbutrin.

SEROTONIN: A neurotransmitter. An imbalance in this chemical is thought to play a role in depression.

STIGMA: In ancient times, a mark of shame. Today it is associated with the shame surrounding mental illnesses such as depression that prevents individuals from seeking treatment.

Bibliography

Aeppel, Timothy. "Ecotherapists Explore the Green Side of Feeling Blue." *Wall Street Journal,* Aug. 14, 1995.

Beck, Aaron. *Love Is Never Enough.* New York: Harper & Row, 1988.

Bower, Bruce. "Growing Up Sad: Depression in Children Attracts Scrutiny." *Science News,* Aug. 5, 1989, pp. 90–91.

Brody, Jane. "Age is No Barrier to Lifting Depression's Heavy Veil." *New York Times,* May 30, 2006.

——. "When Depression Lifts but Sex Suffers." *New York Times,* May 15, 1996.

Brothers, Joyce. "Sharing Traumas Helps in Healing," *Los Angeles Times,* June 2, 1996.

Brown, R. S. "Exercise as an Adjunct to the Treatment of Mental Disorders." In W. P. Morgan and S. E. Goldstone, eds., *Exercise and Mental Health.* Washington, D.C.: Hemipshere Publishing, 1987.

Burns, David D. *Feeling Good: The New Mood Therapy.* New York: Avon Books, 1992.

——. *The Feeling Good Handbook.* Revised Edition. New York: Plume, 1999.

Byrne, A., and D. G. Byrne. "The Effect of Exercise on Depression,

Anxiety, and other Mood States: A Review." *Journal of Psychosomatic Research* 37(1993): 565–74.

Carter, Rosalynn, with Susan K. Golant. *Helping Someone with Mental Illness.* New York: Times Books, 1999.

——. *Helping Yourself Help Others: A Book for Caregivers.* New York: Times Books, 1996.

Consumer Reports. "Mental Health: Does Therapy Help?" November 1995, p. 734.

Cronkite, Kathy. *On the Edge of Darkness: Conversations About Conquering Depression.* New York: Delta Books, 1994.

Eakes, Georgene G. "Chronic Sorrow: The Lived Experience of Parents of Chronically Mentally Ill Individuals." *Archives of Psychiatric Nursing* 9(1995): 77–84.

First, Michael B., Allen Frances, and Harold Alan Pincus. *Diagnostic and Statistical Manual of Mental Disorders.* 4th ed. Washington, D.C.: American Psychiatric Press, 1995.

Fochtmann, Laura J. and Alan J. Gelenberg. "Guideline Watch: Practice Guideline for the Treatment of Patients with Major Depressive Disorder," Second Edition. Arlington, Va.: American Psychiatric Association, 2005.

Freudenberger, Herbert J. "Recognizing and Dealing with Burnout." In Jack Nottingham and Joanne Nottingham, eds., *The Professional and Family Caregiver–Dilemmas, Rewards, and New Directions.* Americus, Ga.: Rosalynn Carter Institute for Human Development, Georgia Southwestern College, 1990.

Glatt, Kenneth M. "Calls Stop Many a Jump off Mid-Hudson Bridge." *New York Times,* Letter to the Editor, Feb. 29, 1996.

Gold, Mark S. *The Good News About Depression.* New York: Bantam Books, 1995.

Goleman, Daniel. *Emotional Intelligence.* New York: Bantam Books, 1995.

——. "Psychologists Dispute Value of Antidepressants," *New York Times,* Nov. 29, 1995.

Gray, D. Patricia. "The Challenge of Caring for the Chronically Mentally Ill," in Jack Nottingham and Joanne Nottingham, eds., *The Professional and Family Caregiver–Dilemmas, Rewards, and New Directions.* Americus, Ga.: Rosalynn Carter Institute for Human Development, Georgia Southwestern College, 1990.

Greist, John H., and James W. Jefferson. *Depression and Its Treatment*. Rev. ed. Washington, D.C.: American Psychiatric Press, 1992.

Herman, Judith Lewis. *Trauma and Recovery*. New York: Basic Books, 1992.

Howitz, Allan V., and Susan C. Reinhard. "Ethnic Differences in Caregiving Duties and Burdens Among Parents and Siblings of Persons with Severe Mental Illness." *Journal of Health and Social Behavior* 36(1995): 138–50.

Jacob, Miriam, Ellen Frank, David J. Kupfer, and Linda L. Carpenter. "Recurrent Depression: An Assessment of Family Burden and Family Attitudes." *Journal of Clinical Psychiatry* 48(1987): 395–400.

Jamison, Kay Redfield. *An Unquiet Mind: A Memoir of Moods and Madness*. New York: Knopf, 1995.

Johnson, Dale L. "The Family's Experience of Living with Mental Illness." In Harriet P. Lefley and Dale L. Johnson, eds., *Families as Allies in Treatment of the Mentally Ill: New Directions for Health Professionals*. Washington, D.C.: American Psychiatric Press, 1990.

Karasu, T. Byram, Alan Gelenberg, Arnold Merriam, and Philip Wang. "Practice Guideline for Treatment of Patients with Major Depressive Disorder," Second Edition. Arlington, Va.: American Psychiatric Association, 2000.

Kazdin, Alan E. "Childhood Depression." *Journal of Child Psychology and Psychiatry* 31 (1990): 121–60.

Kennedy, J. Michael, and Jeff Leeds. "Family, Friends Grapple with Teenagers' Suicides." *Los Angeles Times,* March 19, 1996.

Kramer, Peter D. *Listening to Prozac*. New York: Viking, 1993.

Leary, Warren E. "Depression Travels in Disguise with Other Illnesses," *New York Times,* Jan. 17, 1996.

Lieberman, Abraham. "What You Should Know about Depression in Parkinson Disease." National Parkinson Foundation, 2004.

Maurin, Judith T., and Carlene Barmann Boyd. "Burden of Mental Illness on the Family: A Critical Review." *Archives of Psychiatric Nursing* 4(1990): 99–107.

National Institute of Mental Health, Science Update. "Odds of Beating Depression Diminish as Additional Treatment Strategies Are Needed." November 1, 2006.

Nicoloff, George, and Thomas L. Schwenk. "Using Exercise to Ward Off Depression." *The Physician and Sports Medicine* 23(1995): 44–56.

NIMH Basic Behavioral Science Task Force of the National Advisory Mental Health Council. "Basic Behavioral Science Research for Mental Health: Vulnerability and Resilience." *American Psychologist* 51 (1996): 22–28.

Ornish, Dean. *Love & Survival: The Scientific Basis for the Healing Power of Intimacy.* New York: Harper Collins, 1998.

Oster, Gerald D., and Sarah S. Montgomery. *Helping Your Depressed Teenager: A Guide for Parents and Caregivers.* New York: John Wiley & Sons, 1995.

Podell, Ronald M., with Porter Shimer. *Contagious Emotions: Staying Well When Your Loved One Is Depressed.* New York: Pocket Books, 1992.

Pollin, Irene, with Susan K. Golant. *Taking Charge: How to Master the Eight Most Common Fears of Long-Term Illness.* New York: Times Books, 1996.

Polonsky, William H. *Diabetes Burnout: What to Do When You Can't Take It Anymore.* Alexandria, Va.: American Diabetes Association, 1999.

Rauktis, Mary Elizabeth, George F. Koeske, and Olga Tereshko. "Negative Social Interactions, Distress, and Depression Among Those Caring for a Seriously and Persistently Mentally Ill Relative." *American Journal of Community Psychology* 23 (1995): 279–99.

Rosenthal, N. E., et al. "Seasonal Affective Disorder: Description of the Syndrome and Preliminary Findings with Light Therapy." *Archives of General Psychiatry* 41 (1984): 72–78.

Sargent, Marilyn. *Helping the Depressed Person Get Treatment.* Rockville, Md.: U.S. Department of Health and Human Services, Public Health Service; Alcohol, Drug Abuse, and Mental Health Administration; National Institutes of Mental Health, 1990.

Seelye, Katharine Q. "Remembrance of War: A Personal Dole Emerges." *New York Times,* March 3, 1996.

Shenon, Philip. "President Eulogizes an Admiral with 'a Big Heart,' a Vision and a Deep Sense of Honor." *New York Times,* May 22, 1996.

Solomon, Phyllis, and Jeffrey Draine. "Subjective Burden Among Family Members of Mentally Ill Adults." *American Journal of Orthopsychiatry* 65 (1995): 419–27.

Somer, Elizabeth. *Food and Mood: The Complete Guide to Eating Well and Feeling Your Best.* New York: Henry Holt, 1995.

——. "Food and Mood." *American Health,* April 1995, p. 58.

Spiegel, David and Janine Giese-Davis. "Depression and Cancer: Mechanisms and Disease Progression." *Biological Psychiatry* 54 (2003): 269–82.

Stahl, Stephen M. *Essential Psychopharmacology of Depression and Bipolar Disorder.* New York: Cambridge University Press, 2000.

——. *Essential Psychopharmacology: The Prescriber's Guide: Antidepressants.* New York: Cambridge University Press, 2006.

Styron, William. *Darkness Visible: A Memoir of Madness.* New York: Random House, 1990.

"Technological Tacks to Battling Jet Lag." *Wall Street Journal,* March 1, 1994.

Thiboldeaux, Kim and Mitch Golant. *The Total Cancer Wellness Guide: Reclaiming Your Life After Diagnosis.* Dallas, Tex.: BenBella Books, 2007.

Weissman, Myrna M., et al. "Depressed Parents and Their Children: General Health, Social, and Psychiatric Problems." *American Journal of Diseases of Children* 140 (1986): 801–5.

Wurtman, Judith J. "Depression and Weight Gain: The Serotonin Connection." *Journal of Affective Disorders* 29 (1993): 183–92.

Wurtzel, Elizabeth. *Prozac Nation: Young and Depressed in America.* New York: Riverhead Books, 1995.

Young, Jeffrey E., and Aaron T. Beck. "Cognitive Therapy: Clinical Applications." In A. John Rush, ed., *Short-Term Psychotherapies for Depression: Behavioral, Interpersonal, Cognitive, and Psychodynamic Approaches.* New York: Guilford Press, 1986.

About the Authors

MITCH GOLANT, PH.D., is a clinical psychologist who has been in private practice in West Los Angeles for more than 25 years. He is the Vice President of Research and Development for The Wellness Community National. He is a contributing editor to the *Essentials of Psychosocial Oncology Handbook* (2006) and the author of six books including *The Total Cancer Wellness Guide: Reclaiming Your Life After Diagnosis* (BenBella Books, 2007).

SUSAN K. GOLANT, M.A., is the author or coauthor of more than 30 books on biopsychosocial issues including *Helping Yourself Help Others: A Caregiver's Guide* and the award-winning *Helping Someone with Mental Illness,* both written with former first lady Rosalynn Carter. She has also taught nonfiction writing at UCLA Extension's Writers Program since 1992.